PLAYMAKING

PLAYMAKING

Children
Writing & Performing
Their Own Plays

Daniel Judah Sklar

Teachers & Writers Collaborative
New York

Playmaking

Teachers and Writers is grateful to the following foundations and corporations for their support of our program: American Stock Exchange, Mr. Bingham's Trust for Charity, Louis Calder Foundation, Consolidated Edison, DeWitt Wallace-Reader's Digest Fund, Aaron Diamond Foundation, Joelson Foundatioin, Manufacturers Hanover Trust Company, Mobil Foundation, Morgan Stanley Foundation, New York Telephone, New York Times Company Foundation, Henry Nias Foundation, Helena Rubinstein Foundation, the Scherman Foundation, and the Steele-Reese Foundation. T&W also receives funds from the New York State Council on the Arts, the National Endowment for the Arts, and the New York Foundation for the Arts Artists-in-Residence Program, administered by the Foundation on behalf of the New York State Council on the Arts and in cooperation with the New York State Education Department with funds provided by the National Endowment for the Arts and the Council.

Teachers & Writers Collaborative
5 Union Square West
New York, N.Y. 10003

Library of Congress Cataloging-in-Publication Data

Sklar, Daniel Judah, 1942-
    Playmaking: children writing & performing their own plays /
Daniel Judah Sklar.
        p.   cm.
    Includes bibliographical references
    ISBN 0-915924-34-X.—ISBN 0-915924-35-8 (pbk.)
    1. Children's plays—Presentation, etc.   2. Playwriting—Study and
teaching (Elementary)   3. Children as actors   I. Title.
PN3157.S566   1991   90-37345
792'.0226—dc20   CIP

Printed by Philmark Lithographics, New York, N.Y.
Design: Chris Edgar
Author's Photo: Ellis Hughes

Fourth Printing

TABLE OF CONTENTS

ACKNOWLEDGMENTS

Special thanks to:

Nancy Larson Shapiro and Ron Padgett for initiating and supporting the writing of this book. Ron Padgett for his insightful and scrupulous editing. Chris Edgar for additional editing and design work. Elizabeth Fox and Pat Padgett for support during my various New York residencies for Teachers & Writers Collaborative. Willie Reale and Marsue Cumming for the vision and know-how of the 52nd Street Project. Diane Bath, Suzanne Glennon, Linda Lewis, Susan Long, Tony Long, the Hendrix family, Sally Lovin, Teri Millkey, Nancy Pinaud, and the Georgia Council for the Arts for support during my Georgia residencies. Ann Buckley and Judy Collins, teachers *extraordinaires*. Paula Schwartz and Johnathan Ward for ideas about video and radio. Cassandra Henning for technical support. Elaine Summers and Conrad Bromberg, my teachers, and Laura Maria Censabella and Susan Willerman, my co-workers. John Rainer, *M. le Directeur*. Judy Tate for reading and responding to the manuscript. Mike Seliger for consultation on the bibliography. And Judy Sklar Rasminsky and Zachary Sklar, writers, editors, and friends—as well as sister and brother.

PREFACE

Traditionally, kids have acted in plays written by adults, or—more recently—used Creative Dramatics exercises to improvise their own scenes. In Playmaking too, kids learn to perform scripts and to improvise, but those skills—along with a number of others—lead to a further goal: kids learning to write and perform their own plays.

The emphasis on writing not only develops language arts skills, but it also helps kids to appreciate their own feelings and to use their own imaginations. As Playmaking students write, they explore what they want, what they care about, and what they fear, and they learn how to dramatize those feelings—to create real plays. Producing the plays, in turn, teaches self-discipline, cooperation, and mutual respect.

The emphasis on performance validates the feelings and imaginative flights in the writing. Produced plays win the children the respect and admiration of friends and family as well as teachers and classmates.

The performance also benefits family and friends. These parents, brothers, sisters, buddies, girlfriends, boyfriends, aunts, uncles, and neighbors get to see their own lives and their own communities as their kids do; they get to see themselves reflected—even as they enjoy the writing, acting, costumes, and lights.

This book demonstrates these points by following a prototypical fifth-grade class from its first writing lesson to a full production of its plays. *Playmaking* can be read as a story, or it can be used as a step-by-step guide for teachers. The Brief Lesson Plan (with page references to particular exercises) presents plans for teaching Playmaking in a cycle of twenty weeks.

Each chapter is divided into three parts: 1) a classroom lesson, 2) a discussion between the artist-in-residence, who conducts the lesson, and the classroom teacher, and 3) the artist's reflections on how the lesson and discussion fit into a larger picture.

Playmaking, therefore, is for classroom teachers—particularly those who teach grades 4-12—but it speaks also to parents, theater people, and the general public. Teachers can use it as a drama unit or integrate it into English or social studies. Theater people may see it as a new approach to developing plays. The general public may find the relationship between artists, teachers, and students interesting. In any event, it is a carefully developed and rigorously tested technique for kids writing, acting in, and producing their own plays.

1.

THEATER MAGIC

"Why write a play?" That's the first question I asked the kids at P.S. 34, the Bronx. "Why not a letter or a clear paragraph describing your best qualities?"

"So we can get rich?" answered Hector, a chunky boy of eleven in a turquoise sweatsuit. Hector belonged to Ms. Finney's fifth-grade class, but like many younger kids, he seemed to assume that writing a play is the same as acting in a soap opera and that plays are the same — or poor cousins of—TV shows and movies.

I had to explain that very few people, alas, actually get rich from writing plays.

Maria Margarita, a tall girl who spoke with great precision, said that plays have a "moral." Her tone was dutiful and correct. She sounded like the many students who tell teachers what they want to hear.

I agreed with her, but again asked why she and the others should have to write a play. If they learned to write proper letters and essays, those skills might help them get jobs. But a play?

To my delight, Luz, a pretty girl with long black hair in the second row, said, "It's fun."

"Yes, yes, but why?" I asked. And we began discussing how much fun it is to get up in front of other people and how cool it is to put on a costume and make-up and be someone else.

"What happens when we're being somebody else?" I asked. "What part of ourselves are we using?"

Monique, an intense black girl who sat next to Maria Margarita and whose proper skirt and sweater mirrored the tall girl's, said, "Brain."

"What part of your brain are you using when you make up a story?" I asked.

"Mind," said Hector. He sat just in front of Ms. Finney's extra desk at the back of the room and looked around to see if she had heard his contribution.

"There's a special kind of thinking when we let our minds go, when we make things up. Does anyone know?" I said and waited.

Finally Kim, a light-skinned black girl, who wore a grey, polyester pull-over, said, "Imagination."

"Yes. Writing a play helps develop the imagination," I agreed, "and a healthy imagination will help you sooner or later in life, regardless of whether you become an explorer discovering a new island, a parent breaking up a fight between kids, or a carpenter bracing a building that almost fell in an earthquake. It's how we solve problems when there are no instructions or rules."

The kids, like most other kids—especially teenagers—found that explanation satisfying, so I pressed on. "But why write a play to develop the imagination? Why not a poem? Or a story? Or science fiction? They all use the imagination, don't they?"

The kids agreed guardedly. "So," I persisted, "what's different about a play?"

"The actors," Luz called out. It took a bit more probing for the kids to acknowledge the set designer, lighting person, make-up artist, backstage crew, etc. But once they did, they realized that doing a play means working together. And that it's a way to learn cooperation and discipline.

At that point I recapitulated: "Fun. Imagination. Cooperation. Discipline. Those are all fine goals. If we accomplish any one of them, we will have used our time well. But if we put them together we can do something really special: we can make magic."

This assertion, greeted by smiles at P.S. 34, has elicited cheers, doubtful glances, and even cynical stares at other schools.

My reaction to the smiles was the same as it has been to the stares, glances, and cheers: I showed a video of *The Twins in the Lobby*, written by Erica Hore, an eleven-year-old from Harlem.

In *The Twins in the Lobby*, Sissie and Sally, eleven-year-old twin girls, wait in the hospital lobby while their mother gives birth. Frightened and lonely, the two girls bicker—until Annbellemay, a bag lady, slips into the lobby and teaches them a song and gives them fruit. Annbellemay not only gets them through the wait, she also helps them to understand and appreciate the Annbellemay's of this world.

The P.S. 34 kids loved the video, but when I asked them why, only Kim raised her hand. She said, "It seemed real."

I agreed and asked the other kids if they thought so too. They nodded tentatively, so I asked if they could name a specific part that seemed phony. Monique raised her hand and asked what I meant by "phony," and as I explained, I realized that she and a number of others believed the video was real, a kind of *cinéma vérité*. (It had actually been shot and edited by Teresa Mack and directed by me.) Still others refused to believe a child had actually written the words.

To reinforce the point, I said, "Yes, a child just like you wrote every word. She lives less than twenty blocks from here — five minutes on the subway." As I spoke, my eyes scanned the classroom, finally resting on Jaime, a small boy with a devilish look in his eye.

He cried, "Not me!" as if I had just accused him of running the local crack house.

"Oh yes, you and you and you. Everybody. As I said, you're not only going to write a play, it's going to be magical."

"But how?" asked Kim. The intensity of her expression made me feel that she planned to write her play as soon as I revealed my secret formula.

"That," I said, "is the question I've been waiting for. Can anybody guess the answer?" I paused. Nobody responded.

"The answer is 'honesty,'" I said. "You are all going to explore yourselves — your private worlds.

"That may mean writing about the time you let down your best friend. Or the time you felt so silly that you rolled over and over in the mud or sang the same song fifty times in a row. Or the time you really hated your mother. Or the time you went up on the roof and stayed half the morning, doing nothing...without knowing why. But whatever you choose, it will be yours and yours alone."

"But you said the video wasn't real," said Maria Margarita. Her body seemed to rise in righteous indignation, and I looked down at her feet to see if she had stood. She hadn't, but I noticed how close together the desks were — and how scuffed the floor was.

"The story was made up, but *the feelings* were real. The writer's imagination transformed — does everybody know that word? It means *to change*, like the way you change a transformer toy. So in this case, Erica, the girl who wrote this video, transformed what she felt into a play.

"And that's my job," I continued, "to teach you how to do the transforming. Sometimes the transforming will lead to a serious drama, sometimes to a crazy, wonderful comedy, sometimes to a mystery or a piece of science fiction. But always it will start with you: what you really want, what your bodies, senses, and emotions tell you—what you really feel. What you care about."

"I don't care about writing," said Hector.

"Then maybe you'll write about that: some stupid drama teacher coming in and making you do the most horrible, monstrous task—write about your feelings. You can start with that and maybe it will end with you tricking him and him catching you or not catching you and . . . ."

Hector looked at me carefully.

"Yes, I'm kidding, but I'm also serious. If you write what you really feel, you can't lose. And more than that: we're going to have fun."

"He's crazy," said Jaime quite audibly.

"Maybe. But I'm going to be honest with you—and I'm glad you're already being honest with me.

"You will have to be honest when you act, too," I continued, looking right at Jaime and then at Saul, a big, husky boy in a dark blue sweatshirt with a hood. Saul's eyes darted to the coat closet, which extended from the front door to the back door along the hall-side wall. I imagined him trying to hide among the winter gear when it came time for acting.

"And when you direct. Or design the set or costumes. And if you are honest, you will be saying This is who I am. This is what I believe. So when your parents and friends and neighbors see and hear your play on the stage, they will enter your world. Not Walt Disney's world or even Hans Christian Andersen's. It will be yours, the world of you people in Ms. Finney's class at P.S. 34.

"And that's where the magic comes from: all those people—your parents, friends, and neighbors—learning from you, appreciating you, and discovering what you believe—really embracing who you are. All of them at once."

The kids paid attention, but clearly had difficulty digesting what I said. I was about to try again when Luz raised her hand and said, "Could we see the video again?"

Somehow that made more sense than another explanation. They would be learning this point in action soon enough. So the kids watched the video and I looked out the window of that fourth-floor classroom at a large housing project a few blocks away. In between, all of the buildings had been burned or demolished. I meditated on that scene and my "explanation" until the bell rang.

❦

"I'm a little confused by this 'magic' business," said Ms. Finney. We were depositing fifty cents each in the kitty and getting coffee from the pot in the teachers' lounge. "Is it a good idea to use such words with kids? Especially if I have to do the explaining when you're not here," she added with a wry smile as we sat down. (These weekly sessions, part of an artist-in-residence program sponsored by Teachers & Writers Collaborative, included work with the classroom teacher.)

Looking at Ms. Finney, a handsome woman in her early forties dressed in a grey skirt, white blouse, and a baby blue cardigan sweater, I thought, "You could do this with your eyes closed," but diplomatically replied, "It's all based on a technique with clear exercises."

"Honesty exercises?"

"Oh yes. Most of them are."

"Well," said Ms. Finney, also trying to be diplomatic—not wanting to burst my bubble too abruptly— "where I live in Westchester County, we have a children's theater and it does Creative Dramatics—as well as stunning productions of classics—but it is hardly magic, as nice as it is. I don't think it's wise to set kids up to. . . ."

"Creative Dramatics is only one part of a play written and produced by children," I asserted.

"Don't the kids make things up in Creative Dramatics? Isn't that the point?"

"Yes, but that's just the beginning for a playwright. The playwright starts with the kind of spontaneity that goes into Creative Dramatics games and goes on to writing exercises, which lead to deeper exploration, which leads, in turn, to the writing of the play, which leads, finally, to the production," I said a bit pompously.

Ms. Finney seemed dubious.

"Creative Dramatics nurtures creativity," she said. "Formal plays and elaborate costumes and sets squelch it."

"Think of Creative Dramatics as step number one in a three-step process," I said. "Exploring feelings through games and exercises, writing, and a production." Then I described how one Creative Dramatics exercise had grown into a play.

It was an improvisation done by twelve-year-old boys in an upper middle-class neighborhood of Atlanta, Georgia. Each child had developed a character through Creative Dramatics techniques. As a next step, we agreed to assemble those seven characters, whose ages ranged from six months to seventy-three years, in a rumpus room. We also agreed on a situation: the seven characters would be the male members of a family and they would be setting up a bachelor party for the twenty-three-year-old character. As the improvisation progressed, a conflict between the boy playing the fourteen-year-old and the boy playing his forty-year-old father grew progressively intense and finally overshadowed everything else.

At that point, we agreed that it should be the central conflict for a "real play." The play was then written and rehearsed and finally performed with an extraordinary ending that emerged during the writing: the fourteen-year-old would go to live with his mother.

The mother had not existed in the earlier improvisations, but with time to think and write the boys decided the fourteen-year-old rebelled because his parents had divorced. His confusion about the situation surfaced as rage at his father.

When the kids performed the play, the audience of parents and friends, many of whom were divorced, watched transfixed. And afterwards almost every adult told me they were "shocked" or "chastened" or the like. The kids had started with Creative Dramatics but had taken it much further.

Ms. Finney found that example interesting, but said she had questions. Which she didn't have time to ask; she had to return to class. We agreed to meet after every session. I felt as if I had survived the first cut.

After my talk with Ms. Finney I began thinking about the word *magic*. Was it pretentious, as her tone implied? I was certain that children writing and performing their own plays was different from Creative Dramatics. I also firmly believed in the magic of a truly realized theatrical production. But how could I claim that the kids at P.S. 34 would make magic?

I forgot about that question as I headed home, making my way past a burned-out building in front of which stood young men with their hands in their pockets. They had been there at 8 A.M. when I passed on my way to school.

Not breaking stride, I continued on 138th Street, the bustling main drag of P.S. 34's neighborhood. If I had taken a few more steps I could have entered the subway and headed downtown, but I looked up and saw an espresso machine through the window of La Taza de Azul, a Puerto Rican restaurant. The thought of *cafe con leche* (hot milk and espresso coffee) seemed much more attractive than the subway.

Over the steaming cup, I looked out the window at the shoppers and the tacky Christmas decorations on the store facades, and contemplated the drug supermarket half way between the school and 138th Street.

Unable to make sense of it, I decided to return my attention to "magic," and began reviewing the other places I had taught kids to write plays. It was a long list, including many places in New York City, various towns and cities in Georgia, and a few on the West Coast. But as I thought about the work in each of those places, my eyes kept returning to the street and suddenly I realized why teaching children to explore an impulse and then helping them to develop it into a fully written, fully produced play makes magic: it brings back the first function of the theater, evoking a community.

Today we associate theater with Broadway and its road companies or comfortably established regional theaters — professionals dispensing entertainment to us. Or we imitate what they do with our own amateur companies. Sometimes these plays relate to our lives and we identify with the characters — but always from a distance.

It was different in ancient Greece, in twelfth-century English cathedral towns, and in villages throughout the Third World. Plays emerged from the local community. The writer and his compatriots, who produced and acted in the play, spoke directly to family, friends, rivals, elders, and outcasts. And when all those people came to see the play, they experienced a new understanding of their world. The magic came from the community's embracing and reevaluating itself.

Which is exactly what happens with plays written by children, I thought, and *The Mansion* came to mind.

The Mansion, a mystery drama written by pre-teens, told a story of reclaiming a large abandoned house.

That action, it turned out, mirrored what had happened in Stilson, a farming community of 600 people in south Georgia: as the farm crisis grew and farm after farm failed, the community shrank significantly — until a major highway connected Stilson with Savannah, a city of 200,000.

At that point, ex-farmers began commuting to factory jobs and city people moved to Stilson. The play's action illuminates the changes the people of Stilson faced as they redefined their farming community.

Looking out the window again, I found myself excited by the memory of that powerful play. Or was it anticipation of the plays that would come out of this neighborhood in the South Bronx? Probably both.

2.

SETTING THE TONE

At the beginning of the next session, I announced that we would create a work space by pushing the desks and chairs against the walls. Some of the kids groaned, others waited, but a third group jumped up and began banging chairs and dragging desks as loudly as possible.

"Freeze," I shouted, and everybody did—except Felix.

Felix, a lithe, dark-skinned boy, had gotten up and was sauntering in the direction of the front door. "Is that freezing?" I asked, but Felix kept walking. "You in the green tee shirt. What's your name?"

"Me?" he answered innocently.

"Yes."

"Felix," he said, tossing a crumpled piece of paper into the wastebasket by the front door.

This was clearly going to be a test, so I told the other kids to unfreeze and sit.

"Now, Felix, let me explain something about the theater: when a director tells an actor to freeze, the actor freezes. And if he tells a lighting person to bring up the house lights, the lighting person brings up the house lights. . . . Does everybody know what I mean by 'house lights'?" I said, interrupting myself. Nobody knew, so I, ever anxious to teach, explained that house lights are those that shine upon the audience, not the stage.

"And that's true of everybody else who's part of the theater," I continued. "Do you know why?"

Felix's answer was "I had to throw out some paper."

"Because we count on each other in the theater. For example, let's say Luz is acting"—Luz's smile at this suggestion was love itself—"and she's counting on you to pull the curtain after she says 'And I never want to see you again,' and at that moment you decide you want to throw out some paper or go to the bathroom or joke with your friend. What happens? She's stuck on the stage saying 'And I never want to see you again . . . I never want to see you again . . . I never want to see you again,' till you get back to pull the curtain."

"That's her tough luck," answered Felix. And the kids laughed.

"No, it's yours—because you'd be fired. And do you know why?"

"Because you got it in for me."

"Because you've let her down. You'd have also let down the kids working the lights, the rest of the crew, the director, the playwright, the other actors, and the audience."

Addressing the class as a whole, I said, "We don't let each other down in the theater. We need each other. We count on each other. And if we can't count on you, you go down to the principal's office. We don't waste our time with you."

At that point, Ms. Finney looked up from her desk, where she had been working on her roll book, and said, "Oh, we don't need the principal. We can take care of him right here," and the kids murmured.

"Actually, I wasn't talking about Felix specifically," I said quickly. "Because now that he understands, he won't be doing it again. I meant anybody," and scanned the room.

After that significant pause, I said, "Now we're going to move the desks row by row. When it's your turn, pick up your desk and chair, move them against the nearest wall as quietly as possible, find a spot in the center of the room and stand on it—without talking."

The kids executed these instructions remarkably well, and a twenty-foot by fifteen-foot scuffed wooden work space emerged.

I moved to the center of that space and said, "Now, why do you think I had you move?"

"To waste time," yelled Jaime. "So you don't got to teach nuthin'." He stood near the back of the room. On the wall behind him I noticed the words HARD WORK PAYS OFF in multicolored construction paper.

"Yeah, you just keep us runnin' around," seconded Felix, who stood right in front of me.

"Well, Jaime—and Felix—you may have had teachers like that, but I'm not one and I have a strong hunch Ms. Finney isn't either." The kids giggled nervously. They clearly agreed with my assessment of Ms. Finney.

"So why?" I asked again.

"Man, you ask *why* a lot," said Felix.

"It's my favorite word," I said. "So. . .why?"

Finally Luz raised her hand. "To get more space to act," she said.

"Right, that's definitely part of it. And what else?"

When nobody responded, I said, "To shake you up. Now why would

I want to shake you up?"

"I don't know!" Maria Margarita blurted. Her tone revealed her irritation with such foolishness.

"When you're in your regular seats, you can rely on habits. But when you're out here, you don't know what's next, so you feel more, think quicker, and really use your imagination. All of which makes your writing and acting better."

"It's hard to just stand here," said Deana, a pale, sad-looking girl in jeans and yellow sweater with a gaudy, green flower design. She stood near Ms. Finney's desk at the back of the room and stole a glance at her teacher as soon as the words were out of her mouth.

"Good point. Ordinarily I would have had you sit on the floor Indian style, but so many of the girls are in dresses and...."

"I wouldn't sit on that floor if you paid me," said Tyrone, a short black boy. He was wearing neatly pressed brown slacks.

"Not today, but let's do it next week. Wednesday, a week from today, everybody wear jeans or clothes they can sit on the floor in."

"What does all this have to do with writing a play?" asked Monique, who stood next to Maria Margarita just as she sat next to her in their seats. They, I surmised, worked well in their seats.

I answered Monique by asking her if she remembered what I said last week. Monique dutifully said we would learn to use our imaginations, and we would learn cooperation and discipline.

After complimenting Monique on her memory, I asked, "Does anybody remember anything else?" Nobody did — until Felix said, "Yeah, you said something about magic."

"'Magic,'" mimicked Hector, who stood behind me. I was between him and Felix. Felix said, "What you lookin' at?"

"Nuthin' much," said Hector.

"Hector, what do I mean by 'magic'?" I asked quickly. Hector didn't answer.

"Do you know, Felix?" I asked, switching gears when I saw Felix smirk. He didn't answer either.

"Does anybody remember? What makes the 'magic'?" Nobody responded.

"OK," I said, "the magic comes from honesty about yourself. What you really feel in your heart, what your body tells you, and what you sense with your eyes, ears, nose, mouth, and skin. And sharing all that with an audience. So the question is 'How do we do that? What's the first step?' And the answer, Monique, is that we have to switch the setting—to shake ourselves up. So we'll be alert and open, and so our imaginations will work as well as they can. We will do that every time we work."

"And that's it?" asked Maria Margarita. "Just standing up in the middle of the room will do that?"

"No, once we change the setting, we begin working with our bodies, senses, and feelings. We begin the transforming I told you about last week."

"How do you work with feelings?" asked Kim. She wore the same jeans and pullover as the week before.

"Actually, we're not going to get to feelings today, but that's because feelings are often built upon the body and senses; they help us get to feelings. So we do body and senses first. And of the two, it's best to start with the body. Does anybody know why? No? Then let's think about football. What do you do before you play?"

"Warm up," said Clarence, a tall, rangy black boy, who apparently considered himself the class authority on sports.

"Right. So you get loose. And what happens when you get loose?"

"You move better," said Clarence. He stood still, evenly balanced on his feet, arms dangling. I felt he could have moved effortlessly in any direction.

"And what else? You move better. You're looser, you're focused on what you're doing, you're not worried about anything else. You're what?" I looked at a girl with bright eyes. She wore tan pants and a pretty, beaded blue sweater. Her name was Venus. "What do you think, Venus?" I asked, feeling she had followed the lesson as intently as she had the first day's.

"Relaxed," she said firmly, and then gave me a shy smile.

I smiled back and was about to say "Yes, and when you're relaxed, you can express who you really are," but the bell began ringing and the kids lined up in front of the green chalkboard in the front of the room for a fire drill. I made a mental note to emphasize that link between relaxation and self-discovery, as I followed the kids down the stairs to the street.

❦

"I couldn't help agreeing with Felix on one point," said Ms. Finney when we were sitting in the teachers' lounge later that day.

"Actually, I thought I headed him off quite well."

"Oh you did. Your instinct was absolutely correct there. In fact, it bolsters my point. I was referring to the 'why' business. You do ask that quite a lot."

"It may seem like a contradiction, but when they're loosening up. . . ."

"Yes, I understand all that. But there was a lot of standing around."

"I felt they should understand what they are doing," I said defensively. "I want them to be responsible and you can't do that if you're just following orders."

"We're dealing with a forty-five-minute session," said Ms. Finney, ignoring my whine.

"Less," I thought, remembering the fire drill, but I decided to tell Ms. Finney why moving desks and finding spots in the center was a pallid compromise.

"If I had my druthers, I would do what I did in a private school in Atlanta. I would have the kids take off their shoes and lie flat on their backs. I'd also turn off the light. It would be so much easier for their unconscious impulses to emerge."

Ms. Finney nodded politely and said, "And another practical consideration—Deana, who said she was tired. She is. She lives with her grandmother. They are extremely poor. But more important, when her father died of AIDS, her mother threw herself out the window." Ms. Finney paused and said, "She died too. Deana is exhausted."

The enormity of what Ms. Finney said brought me out of my defensiveness. Teaching in the South Bronx was different from the more affluent neighborhood surrounding Emory University in Atlanta. Worrying about unconscious impulses "emerging" seemed terribly precious. What these kids needed was basic skills to deal with grim realities. I needed to work more directly and let go of the frills. That was what Ms. Finney had been gently telling me.

❦

After Ms. Finney left, I went back to pondering my technique. Was setting a tone an indulgence for the upper middle class? Kids with time and space to slow down and "get in touch" with themselves could benefit enormously from this "professional" approach. But what did it do for kids in the South Bronx? Wasn't their time better spent on fundamentals, as Ms. Finney had hinted? Wasn't I just wasting valuable class time moving furniture? Especially if there wasn't space and a nice soft rug like the one in Atlanta?

On my way home past the burned-out building and its denizens, those questions seemed even more pertinent. I decided to stop for a *cafe con leche* and re-examine the notion of "setting a tone."

Taking the same booth by the window, I thought about how I had set the tone in other inner-city schools. What about the Harlem school where I had taught the previous year?

In that school, we had changed the tone without a rug or proper space, and without moving our chairs to the side of the room (the teacher had preferred that we did not). The kids had stood behind their chairs. But even that small change had distanced the children from the security of their seats. And they had gone on to write wonderful plays like *The Twins in the Lobby*. Their teacher, who clearly distrusted me as yet another "specialist," agreed the plays worked and even said that after the playwriting section the kids seemed to like writing—some for the first time.

Taken by itself, this example proved little, but it reminded me why I developed the technique. I had designed it to appeal to non-readers and non-writers as well as the speedy, the plodding, and the average. "Shaking the kids up" puts everybody on an equal plane. Non-readers and plodding readers can perform as well as anybody else. Equally important, the non-readers feel motivated to learn: after they are shaken up, they go on to create scenes through improvisation and other theater games. That, in turn, leads to an interest in grammar and spelling, because they realize those skills will help them build their improvisations into plays.

So an interest in writing skills often depends upon the success of the improvisations. And good improvisations often happen after a break from traditional classroom thinking. That's why I try to shake the kids up, why I set a special tone.

3.

FOUNDATION

The next week, after we had found our spaces on the floor, I said, "OK, now we're going to work on breathing." Thirty-two bemused faces looked back at me. "Yes," I continued undaunted, "we're going to practice what you do every day, all day long. Does anybody know why?"

I found myself looking at sixty-four unraised hands, so I said, "How many people in this class have given an oral report?" Almost every child raised a hand. "And of you who raised your hands—how many have felt as if his or her voice might crack? Or hands might shake? Or began to sweat?" Many raised their hands again. "Nervousness can be controlled by breathing. Breathing properly helps us to relax," I said.

"So that's why we do it first," said Luz, whose long black hair had been pulled back into a tight pony tail. She was wearing jeans and a black sweatshirt.

"Right, when we pay attention to our breath, we can then begin to use our muscles, senses, and even our feelings in a new way."

"And our minds?" said Maria Margarita. She and Monique, dressed again in skirts and sweaters, stood in front of the science laboratory area in the very back of the room. That day it housed a family of gerbils.

"Yes," I acknowledged, "but that's in the next part of the work. If we use our minds right away, we sometimes ignore our bodies, senses, and feelings."

"When I write I use my mind," said Maria Margarita, who tried to stare me down.

"Try it this way first, Maria Margarita. You can always go back to your way later," I said to her stony face. "This might give you another option, another choice. Another way of working."

Maria Margarita remained unmoved, but I asked everybody to raise their hands above their heads and inhale anyway. And then I said, "Bring your hands down toward the floor and exhale slowly." When their hands were half way down, I asked them to bend their knees as they continued dropping their hands and exhaling. When their hands reached the floor, I told them to let the last bit of breath escape.

Some of the kids tried to touch the floor without bending their knees. Others rushed. Still others forgot about the breathing. But a good half had done it correctly. And it became obvious that Elizabeth, who stood in front of me in jeans and a longsleeved orange tee shirt, moved with consummate grace.

The next inhalation happened while they remained with their heads down, hands on the floor, and knees bent. The exhalation started there too, but as the breath escaped I asked the kids to straighten their knees— but leave every other muscle as it was. The result was a good stretch for the hamstrings.

More of the kids got this stage of the exercise. It seemed as if they realized that speed worked against them, that they were going into uncharted territory and it would be wise to follow my instructions. At that point I noticed how Clarence seemed as perfectly balanced with his head down as he had the previous week standing in a position of his choice.

The last inhalation began as they bent their knees and slowly raised their arms up over heads again and stood. On the last exhalation the arms came down to the sides—without slapping.

I emphasized "without slapping" so that I could focus on the issue of control again. After such an elaborate set of instructions, children often want to slap as loudly as possible. But I asked them to resist that impulse because we were learning to relax and remain in control at the same time.

Still, when the whole cycle was done, I heard a slap. So, I told the kids we would do the cycle again, an announcement that elicited groans. But I said, "We'll keep doing it till it's perfect. And you guys know why."

"I don't," cried Felix in his bright red tee shirt.

"Does Luz being on the stage and you not pulling the curtain ring any bells?" I asked. Felix and I smiled directly at each other.

"Yes, but if one kid makes a mistake, I still don't see why we should all pay," said Monique.

"Think about us as an orchestra," I said, borrowing an image from Konstantin Stanislavsky, the Russian director who created Method Acting. "Each of you is an instrument. If you're not tuned properly or if you play your note at the wrong time—or you don't play your note—the whole piece of music sounds bad. The same with a play."

That seemed to make sense to the kids, so I pursued the image. "And that's why we warm up the body. It's part of our instrument. Just as the senses are. And our feelings."

The kids did the breathing cycle correctly twice. But on the third time, Hector slapped and I said we would do it till it was perfect again. That brought cries of outrage, but I said it was a matter of being writers and actors as opposed to just kids.

"When you work with me, you are not just kids, you are actors and writers. Professionals. And I expect professionals to do their work."

The next cycle went perfectly, so I introduced a second breathing exercise: I asked the children to lace their hands, take a deep breath, and stretch their hands above their heads. When they had exhaled, they brought their hands down and placed them on their heads. On the second inhalation they raised their hands again but on the exhalation they brought their hands to the "praying position."

We did that cycle four times. I felt as if they had slowed down and focused, so I asked them what they felt.

After a pause, Venus did an encore. "Relaxed," she blurted out and the others murmured assent. It was time to loosen muscles.

"Now we're going to take inventory of your muscles," I said. "Does everybody know what 'inventory' means? It's what a grocery store manager does when he counts how many boxes of Froot Loops he has on the shelf. He does that to decide what he's going to order when the supply man comes. We're going to see which muscles need a new supply of air and exercise."

"So close your eyes and listen to your body: how do your toes feel? Are they relaxed, tense, itchy? How about calves, thighs, belly, lower back, chest, upper body, shoulders, arms, neck, and head?" I said, going slowly, allowing the children to listen to their bodies, making it a time for privacy.

Most of the kids responded to this opportunity enthusiastically. Like teenagers and adults, they reveled in the delicious sense that their job as students obliged them to pay attention to themselves.

Watching the class, I noticed that some children clearly felt a special affinity to their bodies, but Deana seemed to experience the exercise as another chore. And Saul and Hiram, another big boy who always wore a jean jacket, seemed self-conscious. I made a mental note to pay special attention to those three.

When we were done, I asked the kids to choose the part of their bodies that felt least comfortable (maybe the tummy before lunch or a knee sore from falling on the playground or necks and shoulders stiff from too much desk sitting) and to breathe into it; to sense how the air radiated from their lungs to the hurt muscle. Jaime said every muscle in his body felt great, so I asked him to breathe into his tummy for fun. Some of the boys — Saul and Hiram and two other buddies in the back of the room, Victor and Benny — had difficulty sensing how the breath flowed, but many of the other kids discovered how they could focus their breath and even get relief from pain. I made a mental note to repeat this often and if necessary to work with those boys privately.

To go from doing inventory and maintenance of the muscles to stretching them — and to change the tone a bit — I taught the following game: I told the kids they would be seven feet tall, as tall as Patrick Ewing. All they had to do was concentrate on the little bones piled upon one another that we call vertebrae. The vertebrae, I explained, make up the backbone but are attached by tendons and ligaments; it is not continuous bone. The children could stretch the space in between if they concentrated.

Felix tried to go on his toes but I assured him that the real stretch is in the backbone and urged him to concentrate there. "Anybody can go on his toes," I said. "I want you to be in charge of your backbone."

Once they knew the fun of imagining and stretching, I asked them to scrunch to dwarf size, reminding them again that the real work is in the backbone, not in bending the knees. The excitement rose when we expanded to the sides without stretching our arms out; we took the muscles on either side of the backbone and our buttocks and our shoulders and separated them. And, finally, we hugged the backbone so that we could be skinny enough to go through a keyhole.

I decided to take the offensive with Ms. Finney in discussing body work. "How do you think Maria Margarita took to my downplaying the mind?" I asked.

She looked at me carefully. "I don't know about her, but I spend a lot of time urging these children to think. They have abundant opportunity to 'listen to their impulses.'"

"Ah yes, but that's just self-indulgence," I said quickly. "The way we do it they're learning to make impulses into the *lesson*; they're working with those impulses, not being their victims. As you can see, the thing I keep stressing is control."

"That's all well and good, but I wonder if they understand what you're saying," said Ms. Finney, and for the first time I sensed an undercurrent of hostility.

"I think they understood," I said defensively.

"I don't think they understood 'erratic breathing will subvert creative impulses,'" said Ms. Finney, pulling out a sheet of paper where she had recorded the phrase.

"Well, I'm glad you're listening," I said with a smile. And when that smile was greeted with silence, I added, "And you're right about the theater jargon. A little jargon works well with high school students, but not at the elementary level."

When she still didn't respond, I said, "How did you feel about that appeal to professionalism on the control issue? I find kids of any age, but especially pre-teenagers, like to be treated as people doing a job and—"

"On the one hand you're asking them *why* all the time and then you're saying don't think."

Feeling I was being tested much the way I had been tested by Felix, I said, "I'm trying to create a context where they can be both spontaneous and under control."

"That's a contradiction," said Ms. Finney as she stood to get more coffee. I noticed her handsomely cut tweed suit as she walked to the pot.

"Not necessarily," I said to her back, and began to describe how I used standard calisthenics with a group of eleven-year-old boys who had previously shunned acting as "sissy." These farm boys in Brooklet, Georgia, had made fun of each other at the first session when I began with breathing, but at the second, I started with calisthenics and the boys began working. And when the lesson moved onto more "arty" exercises, these same boys stayed with me, creating wonderful characterizations of coon dogs, "King Kong" vehicles, and other, more imaginative choices. They even stayed when we moved on to playwriting, becoming the cornerstone of a playwriting project that evolved into a major school presentation.

Ms. Finney remained unmoved, so I pressed on. "The key is to create a context, so that the exploration will be free but not out of control. I did the same thing in a school not far from here. . . ."

"That's why you've put off the thinking."

"Yes, they'll be thinking like crazy later on."

"All right," said Ms. Finney. This was not assent; she had had enough of my harangue.

"And one last thing," I said, as Ms. Finney stood, "if these impulses find a direct positive outlet, they won't appear as 'acting out.' And all the while, the kids are gaining better control of their bodies, senses, and feelings. They're becoming truly sophisticated."

Ms. Finney said, "I've got class," and left.

At home that night, I decided to do some body work of my own, some Kinetic Awareness exercises.

Elaine Summers, the creator of Kinetic Awareness, inspired me to make body work the first step on the way to acting in or writing a play. She showed me how we store feelings in particular parts of our bodies and when we slow down and feel those parts, we're reminded of our feelings. So, for example, a trauma with one's mother could be associated with the time she pinched an arm. The body stores the memory of such shocks.

According to Kinetic Awareness, those suppressed feelings can be discovered by the kinds of things we had done in class today: the breathing, the inventory, the stretching game. They help us pay attention to the self that's always being checked, held back, repressed.

Suddenly, I wished I could just call up Ms. Finney and tell her about Kinetic Awareness. I had felt so defensive in the teachers' lounge. I had emphasized the body as a "hook" without emphasizing how essential it is to any artistic work. I also wanted to tell Ms. Finney about Elaine and how she had helped me to enjoy my body, emphasizing the pleasure in slowing down and paying attention; about Elaine's ability to cut through the easy assumptions we Americans make about our bodies as well as the dogmas of other exercise techniques and Eastern cults. And how that pleasure and clarity prepared a foundation for creative work.

At our next session I would not only tell Ms. Finney about Elaine but also credit the other exercises: the first two breathing exercises I learned from a yoga technique taught by Martin Pierce, a wonderful teacher in Atlanta, and the "inventory-taking" technique came from Elaine. Also I would tell her about Konstantin Stanislavsky's *An Actor Prepares,* a book that not only influenced my ideas about acting and writing but also about teaching and how to write about it.

But what I wanted to tell her most was about my experience at Park West High, a Manhattan alternative school. My three sessions there seemed to crystalize all we had been saying about control and freedom.

Park West is a special school. The teenagers there have all been kicked out of two other schools. There is a school nursery for the students' babies. And, as one might imagine, the kids distrusted me — as well as almost everybody else.

At first they resisted the breathing warm-ups, but a few tried them and the others finally followed suit. So I decided against the stretching game. The Park West kids, like the kids I had described to Ms. Finney, had responded well to the discipline of the breathing work and I wanted to offer a similarly exacting stretch for the spine. We did a "hang-out" (another Summers exercise).

I told them that as actors and writers their bodies had to be flexible as well as relaxed. And that the best place to start is the backbone. To imagine the vertebrae and stretch the space between them by "hanging out"; by starting at the base of the skull and slowly stretching the space between each of the vertebrae in the neck by dropping the head to the chest in six stages; from there letting the shoulders go, stretching the space between each of the vertebrae in the upper back; the same for the middle back by rounding the spine "like a cat"; and finally stretching the vertebrae in the lower back and allowing the whole neck and torso to hang free. The exact stretch in reverse leads them back to standing.

We also did an inventory, but when I worked with the teenagers, I told them how lucky they were; that this would be a time to be "self-indulgent." The Park West High kids giggled at this notion but, like Ms. Finney's kids, soon were seduced by the luxury of listening to themselves on officially sanctioned time.

When we finally got down to writing at Park West High, extraordinary work emerged. In the most interesting play, *Card,* a girl rents her

Medicaid card for $100 to her best friend, so that the friend can have an abortion. That play elicited the most passionate debate I have ever witnessed. The moral issues erupted: friendship, family obligations, and the right of a woman to choose. How many times had that group of children learned about the dangers of teenage pregnancy? How many times had they sat dully through such lectures? But here they were galvanized by a truly felt, beautifully rendered play by a girl with barely adequate English skills.

I do not claim that this vital play emerged only because the girl had done some yoga breathing, executed a "hang out" and taken an inventory of her body. But the body work at the Park West sessions helped her and the rest of the kids to listen to their impulses *and* to bring them under control; to create a balance between discipline and freedom. And that balance provided a foundation for truly satisfying creative work.

I wanted Ms. Finney to realize that I had been aiming for that balance when I stopped Felix and when I cut Maria Margarita off. It also was behind the repetition of the breathing exercises and the attention to detail as we took inventory of our bodies. It would become the foundation for the rest of Playmaking.

4.

CHOICE

Most children memorize the Five Senses in the second or third grade. They also, of course, understand seeing, hearing, touching, tasting, and smelling. But few connect the lesson with everyday experiences. Fewer still realize they can control those experiences. And almost none understand that memories of those feelings make their acting and writing fuller and richer. To facilitate that leap, I started "sense work" with a game.

The game, a variation of Statues (the traditional kids' game), starts with each child on his or her spot. "On that spot, you can jump and hop and twist as much as you like," I said, once the P.S. 34 kids had positioned themselves. "But you can't step off it or yell (it might disturb other classes) and you must stop when I say 'freeze.' Freeze in whatever position you find yourself." When I said "Go," the kids jumped and twisted with abandon, and when I yelled "Freeze," they froze beautifully. While they were frozen, I told them to close their eyes and imagine that they had become a statue made of steel, not flesh and blood. Without changing the pose, they rigidified into steel. And, when I released them, they jumped again. Only to freeze moments later. And become statues made of cotton candy, jello, rubber, and so on.

The kids truly enjoyed this game. Only Tyrone, who remained concerned about the press in his slacks—blue this time—resisted. I told him he could sit on the side. There, scrunched in a chair that had been pushed against the wall below the public address speaker near the front of the room, he became restless and after a while joined in. His point, I gathered, had been made. Why miss the fun?

Meanwhile I let a few of the kids choose the substance. Elizabeth chose cardboard; Luis, a short boy with a shock of black hair, plastic (I would later discover Luis loved technology); and William, a skinny light-skinned black boy, wood. I closed the game with ice cream statues melting. "Melting," I explained, "is hard work. Any little kid can fall down. But an actor needs to be strong and in control to melt s-l-o-w-l-y."

At that point I explained the word *actor*. Theater professionals use *actor* to refer to both males and females. The word *actress*, while used by some in theater and many in film and TV, creates an unfortunate division. Boys and girls do the same exercises and I treat them the same, just as I would professional male and female actors. The term *actor* thus bestows a measure of dignity and respect. It reminds the students that they are not just little kids or girls or boys but actors and writers working at a craft.

I also squeezed a short "trip" into that session. "Your favorite aunt from Chicago has just come to town and she's promised to take you to the beach," I said. "Take a moment and tell me three things: what kind of car does she drive? What is she wearing? And how are you dressed?"

The exercise allows the children to choose. In Macon, Georgia, for example, the car of choice tended to be the Lamborghini, and the BMW got a lot of votes in one section of Atlanta. But in the South Bronx, Cadillac led the field.

Additional choices followed: I asked them to decide the car's color, its model, its year, and the number of doors it had. I also asked how the aunt dressed. Did her dress have a full skirt? Did her shoes match her dress? And of course the child's own clothes: what kind of sneakers? Reebok? And what color? High top, low top?

Once the children clearly imagined these details, the traveling began. I asked them to imagine that the aunt had just pulled up, to take hold of an imaginary door handle, swing open the door, and slide into an imaginary seat.

The kids mimed those movements well, so I asked, "What happens next?" "I drive," said Felix, and he started to zoom towards the large standing globe between Ms. Finney's desk and the science laboratory. I stopped him with a "freeze" and then I asked, "Why did I stop him?" Maria Margarita, who wore a blue jump suit that day (as a sort of compromise, I imagined), pointed out that his aunt sat at the wheel.

"Right," I agreed, "you are in the passenger seat. Now, what do you have to do before she'll start driving?"

Maria Margarita started to answer but Luz spoke quicker. "Seat belts," she said. We all buckled up and mimed riding along in the passenger seat.

As we traveled, I said, "Your aunt is in a good mood and she's going to let you play the radio. Where is it?" Hector reached directly in front, but Kim, who wore a different top but the same old jeans, accepted the reality of being a passenger in the front seat and reached forward and left.

Once the others had found the dial, I asked them to imagine a song. Not just the artist, but a specific song, and within that, specific notes and lyrics. If certain children couldn't remember any other song, I asked them to hear "Jingle Bells."

Luz chose "Da Butt" and others followed suit. Which I allowed. "Just as long as you hear it in your own head," I said. So we started moving, each child humming and moving (within the limits of seat belt and seat)—pausing only to open a window or turn on air conditioning.

Before we reached the beach, we stopped for ice cream. The kids chose flavors, and I asked them to listen to the radio, feel the breeze, and eat the ice cream all at once. Luz and Venus seemed to imagine and coordinate the three senses the most naturally, but almost all the kids enjoyed the game. It seemed a good point to stop. (The next lesson we actually reached the beach and felt the hot pavement of the parking lot—with those oases, the cooler white lines—the warm sand, the cold water. . . .)

I asked the kids how many senses we used on our trip and where we used them. Maria Margarita and Monique raised their hands immediately, but I called on Jasmine, a shy child who seemed delicate in her new, stiff jeans. She answered correctly and confidently. I let Maria Margarita and Monique give other examples.

I also emphasized how an actor or writer or any creative artist must be clear about details. Details make the difference between excitement and boredom. A performer who really sees the red of his Cadillac or one who feels the smoothness of her silk blouse interests us. The one who sees only a car or clothing remains vague and uncompelling.

Ms. Finney complimented me on the Statues game but also said, "Don't they have enough of that already?" meaning talk of Lamborghinis and songs like "Da Butt."

Having agonized over this question on my own, I responded quickly. "Actually, the exercise does the opposite. In breaking the car or outfit into component parts, the kids redefine those material goods; they make BMWs into the building blocks of art; instead of feeling in awe of Lamborghinis, they use them. So at first the material images make art seductive, but soon the *process* becomes attractive."

"Well, that sounds good," said Ms. Finney. She had followed my logic but remained dubious. "But all that emphasis on brand names. . . . Even if you're 'redefining' them, it's still a commercial."

"No, they are just more details. Like the heat of the day or the smells in the air. The writer or actor or artist learns to pay attention to them and trust his or her memory.

"This whole approach," I continued, "stems from the work of Stanislavsky, that Russian director and actor I mentioned before. He calls it Sense Memory and it is the cornerstone of the Method."

I could tell Ms. Finney wanted to change the subject, so I explained that Stanislavsky's technique had been taught to our greatest actors, from Marlon Brando, Marilyn Monroe, and Paul Newman to Al Pacino, Ellen Burstyn, Dustin Hoffman, and Robert De Niro.

"I thought this was writing class," she answered ironically. Her elegant grey wool dress made her look particularly sure of herself.

"Writing and acting and painting and every other art grow from details," I said. "I'm teaching them to work as artists, to discover themselves by discovering what details interest them, their choices." And then I described Candy.

Candy, a pre-teen from Stilson, Georgia, created a character named Penny the Pecan. Penny had fallen from a tree. The image, Candy told me, came to her as a memory of lying in the grass under her grandfather's big tree. Candy went on to write about the separation and loneliness that moment evoked. It became a wonderful play.

"And you're going to do this with my kids?" she asked, standing up.

"Oh yes, these exercises and acting are just steps on the way to writing a play."

Ms. Finney nodded politely, turned on her high heels, and went back to class.

❧

After Ms. Finney left, I sat in the lounge and wondered if her children could do Sense Memory work. Some certainly could. But others needed to build upon the exercises I do with younger children before exploring specific memories.

For example, younger children respond well to exercises where they handle imaginary objects. I often ask them to build an "imaginary shelf," a game I adapted from an exercise in Viola Spolin's wonderful book *Improvisation for the Theater*. Some kids build the shelf with their hands, others create imaginary hammers and nails and saws, some sit there saying "This is stupid." But soon enough they build the shelf, at which point I ask them to put five imaginary objects on it: a globe, a feather duster, a pair of bronzed baby shoes, a vase with a rose in it. When those objects are in place, I ask for a volunteer to take his or her objects off the shelf in front of the whole class—only in a mixed-up order. The class must guess the order in which the objects are removed. The volunteer "wins" when the class guesses correctly.

On the other hand, the more sophisticated pre-teens and teenagers can do Sense Memory as it works in the Method. For example, I would say, "Remember a time your mother grounded you and left you alone in your room. Explore all the sensual experiences of that moment. Was the room hot? Where was your mother standing? What was she wearing? Could you smell her perfume?" After a few moments, I ask the student to mime the moment, incorporating the answers to all those questions.

Often when students mime for the first time, they may revert to telegraphing the sensations by using cliches like shaking a fist to indicate anger or putting two fingers to the nose to indicate a bad smell. But when asked to slow down, they experience those memories sensation by sensation and they remember how they moved, what they thought, what they did with their hands. Which brings the scene to life.

Having juxtaposed the imaginary shelf and the Sense Memory exercises, I suddenly realized what united them: choice. In these and the other sense exercises, the children learn to pay attention to their impulses and to assert them as choices.

At that point, a group of teachers came into the lounge, so I went to La Taza de Azul to continue my meditation on choice and plan my "sense strategy" for Ms. Finney's class.

Once at my table, I refocused on choice. The beauty of sense work—and acting and writing in general—comes from approval. Sense exercises, like the rest of the technique, encourage children to trust themselves; each time a Felix discovers that his six-tiered shelf interests his friends and teacher, or a Candy senses that others respond to her loneliness, they feel more confident. They see that other people value their choices, their specialness.

At that point, I realized that I would do as much sense work with Ms. Finney's kids as time allowed. We would try Sense Memory as well as the imaginary shelf and the trips. And we would return to it all semester. Choice seemed that important.

5.

USING IT

Children often express their feelings more directly than adults but they are also quicker to lose control, often allowing the feelings to feed upon themselves, creating chaos, making listening impossible, and sometimes causing serious disturbance. As actors and writers, children learn to develop, harness, and enjoy their feelings.

Theater games make the harnessing process not only feasible but also fun. At P.S. 34 we started with a variation of Sound and Motion, another game developed by Viola Spolin and described in her *Improvisation for the Theater*.

This Sound and Motion game began with all the children forming a circle. I chose Luz to walk to the center first. Before she started, I told her to respond to whatever I said with one sound and one motion. The sound could not be a word, only an emotionally laden sound. When she reached the center, I said, "Your daddy just kissed you on the forehead" and Luz responded with "Icckkkkk" and a violent wipe of her forehead. "Now keep making that sound and doing that motion," I told her. When she established a rhythm, I told her to pick another student and walk over to him or her while continuing to wipe and ickkkkk. When Luz was in front of Venus, Venus's sparkling eyes took in the icckkkkk and the wipe and she began to imitate them. When Venus had copied them correctly (she started with her right hand—Luz had been doing it with her left), I told her to do them with Luz three more times and then walk past her to the center, continuing to icckkkkk and wipe. I told Luz to take Venus's place in the circle. When Venus reached the center, I told her she got all A's on her report card. "Ohhhhhhhh!" she cried and threw her hands up in the air, a wonderful, elated movement. She repeated this motion and sound until she had a rhythm and then gave it to Deana. Deana, shy at first, began copying Venus, and when I said "You just smelled fresh, baked bread," she said, "Mmmmmmmm" and raised a fist to her mouth.

This game, which has never failed to charm and thrill any group of kids (or adults), can develop in a number of ways. Children can take the teacher's place offering emotional triggers. ("Your boyfriend took out your best friend," one teenager said to a rival.) Or the children can take the sound and motion and move to the center and keep repeating it until a kinetic impulse tells them to vary it, which is the way Spolin does Sound and Motion.

From Sound and Motion we moved to improvisation. Stanislavsky and his disciples use improvisation extensively. Improvisation also serves as the cornerstone of Creative Dramatics. Spolin (as well as other advocates of Creative Dramatics) provides numerous situations to improvise. The following technique draws upon both Stanislavsky and Spolin.

I begin by asking two children to come forward. Usually it's two girls, but in this group, the dynamic between Hector and Felix interested me. Their rivalry, I thought, could be built upon and ultimately diffused. So I asked them both to come forward.

Once they were in front, I told Hector to go outside. Alone with Felix, I told him his name would be "Mike." When the improvisation began, "Mike" would enter the hallway after school and see "Bill," who would be played by Hector. Everybody else would be gone, so "Mike" would take a ball out of his book bag and toss it to "Bill." "Bill" would throw it back and they would play ball until "Bill" tossed the ball so high that it broke a light. Once that happened, I explained to Felix, he had to talk "Bill" into going to the principal and explaining what had happened. Running away would only make things worse, I emphasized. He had to get "Bill" to admit his mistake. I asked Felix if he could do that. He said he could.

Then I asked him to go out and send Hector in. I explained the same thing to Hector, but instead of telling him to go to the principal, I told him to get "Mike" to run away. "Nobody saw," I said. "You have been in trouble before. If you get caught it will be bad. And you can't leave him. He could tell." I then told them to make up the scene as they went along, with only one limitation: they could not hit each other.

Hector and Felix improvised beautifully. Hector offered Felix fifty cents. Felix threatened to tell Hector's mother. They became so involved that when I motioned to Monique to play teacher, they responded to her question—"What's going on here?"—with genuine spontaneity, each immediately laying the blame on the other. Later on, when they went to the office (the principal was played by Maria Margarita) and especially when their parents came, they got a little hammy. But those first moments really worked.

The improv grew until the parents of "Bill" accused the parents of "Mike" of being a bad influence and I cut it off, saying, "Take out a fresh sheet of paper and write what happened to each character in the end." They could do it in prose, I assured them.

This step crossed the dividing line between Creative Dramatics and playwriting. The children began to think and write as opposed to just responding and evolving material as a group. They created endings that bespoke their individual feelings. The results were fascinating:

—Victor, who had been uninterested in almost everything else up to this point, said, "Mike's parents"—who had been played as wild, self-justifying boors by William and Elizabeth—should pay for the light because they "brought him up bad." The boys should *not* be punished, only be warned by the principal and watched by the teacher.

—Deana said the boys should have counseling with the school psychologist.

—Kim, whose response was three pages long, meted out after-school cleaning as punishment for the boys. It also indicated that "Juan" the janitor, played by Luis, would supervise them. The two sets of parents would see the school counselor. The principal and teacher would have a faculty meeting about the problem.

The two-girl improvisation begins the same way. I call up two girls and ask one to go outside. To the first girl I say, "You are a teenager who has just been given her own room for the first time. It's your private space. You can do anything you want there. You don't bother your parents in their space and you expect them to respect your privacy and style in yours. Now, it just so happens you're a little sloppy. There is, for example, a candy wrapper on the floor and some underwear on a chair—but that's your business. Nobody can tell you how to keep your room. You have to stand up for your right to keep it the way you want. Even when your mother badgers you, as she has been doing lately."

The girls then switch places and I tell the second girl she is the mom. "You have spent three months getting this new apartment just the way you want it. Today your husband's parents are coming over to see it for the first time. Everything is in order but your daughter's room. You have to go in there and make her clean it up. You can't hit her (one of my cardinal rules), but you may bribe her or ground her or beg her or do whatever you think will get her to clean up the room."

At that point I call the daughter back and have her begin a phone conversation about some cute guy at school. Once she starts speaking, Mom knocks and they proceed to improvise. The variations are infinite. Grounding, name calling, shaming, etc. Sometimes the actors even reach a compromise. But regardless of what they do, I ask them to freeze after a few minutes and take suggestions from the rest of the class. "You are now playwrights," I explain. "You must tell the actors how to end the scene." The actors listen to the playwrights, try a few of the suggestions, and then choose one.

At that point I ask the mom and daughter to go outside, so that I can explain to the boy playing Dad that he has to find out what's happening between them. Often boys will back the mom vociferously, so I usually tell the boy his wife is overreacting. His own parents are not as fussy as she. He's to defend his daughter. If this scene is not resolved by actors, I bring in the playwrights again.

Grandma and Grandpa's entrance comes next. These grandparents, I explain to the boy and girl playing the parts, love their granddaughter without qualification. She can do no wrong. They might even clean her room for her! But if not that, they will certainly have opinions about her upbringing. When that scene develops, I stop the actors and ask everybody in the class to devise his or her own ending, among which have been:

—The girl goes to live with her grandparents and the parents get a divorce.

—The mother and grandmother get in a fight and the girl never sees the grandparents again.

—The girl sneaks out the window and goes off with her boyfriend.

—The girl cleans up her room to avert a break between grandparents and parents.

"Well, well, well," said a smiling Ms. Finney. "That was an exciting session."

I luxuriated in her approval, but soon became uneasy as she went on describing how *therapeutic* it was for Felix to play the "good" child and Hector the "bad." And how the whole experience was a controlled "acting out" of anti-social behavior, which therefore vitiated that behavior. And how it also would give the children poise. She had seen the same thing in the Creative Dramatics in her Westchester town.

I agreed with her, but felt uneasy. She said nothing about the writing. So I explained that I would now choose five of the children's endings and have the children act those. I would make the choices on the basis of originality, completeness, and willingness to put the endings in proper play form. That way I would use their excitement and interest to get them writing.

"By engendering competition," she interjected. "As if they don't get enough of that in sports and the street itself."

Suddenly I, who had enjoyed the praise and then gone on to lecture, felt caught up short. "Yes, there are definite elements of that," I said. "I mean ideally we should do everybody's ending. And, by the end of the term, everybody will have a turn, but time and space and. . . ."

"We want the children's interest, but we needn't pander to it," she said.

Struggling to defend myself, I cited a group of fourth graders in another South Bronx school. Many of them had trouble writing. They had difficulty focusing on a page for more than a few seconds, according to their teacher. But when they wrote to present their vision of the problem to their peers, they sat and focused. And those who did not have their plays read aloud got to act in others. Or controlled the lights. Everybody participated. When we had finished, their teacher said that not only were they writing better but that they seemed to read and participate more.

"I would think that would be true for those whose plays were done," said Ms. Finney, "but what about those whose plays 'lost'? I wonder how their confidence fared."

"They wrote full plays. And then they got the satisfaction of acting or working backstage," I said hotly.

"Yes, you've said that," she said and stood. That day she wore a proper brown suit and I decided, as I watched her leave, that it reflected her rigidity.

❧

The whole notion of competition bothered me more than I would admit, and later that week, I wondered if I had subverted all I had been doing by "pandering" to competition. Was my real lesson "dog eat dog"? Had my need to interest kids eclipsed the work?

As the doubts continued to tumble in, I tried to think of other ways I had solved the problem. In an unruly Manhattan class that had lost two teachers in half a term, I had the children write two-character plays in pairs, having each child responsible for one character's part of the dialogue. I also had helped Georgia kids create "group plays" by improvising and recording those improvisations. Both of those techniques had worked, but, finally, each child had contributed only a part of the vision.

Had I ever allowed each child to create and fulfill a vision? No. In most situations I had let every child write, but reverted to competition for the productions. And just chalked it up to lack of time. Now that stop-gap choice seemed not only glaringly inadequate but potentially harmful. Hadn't one pre-teen in Atlanta refused to say hello to me when I chose her as a producer of another child's play instead of doing hers? How many others had suffered quietly?

We simply had to do everybody's play, but how would we find the time? Maybe I could ask Ms. Finney to do productions in the last twenty minutes of the day. I wouldn't be there but I could read them . . . . Somehow that solution fell short as well. I seemed to be stuck with competition — and not happy about it.

My confusion about competitiveness remained until I went to a Teachers & Writers Collaborative meeting later in the week. The meeting of artists-in-residence working all over New York City concerned the problem of correcting grammar as opposed to using the imagination.

Almost everybody argued that our job, as artists, was to teach the kids how to use the imagination. If we had time to teach grammar as well, wonderful. But first things first.

I agreed with the majority and when there was a pause, I raised the issue of competition. There were many responses, but none felt like the answer. What proved most helpful was the sense that each of these other artists-in-residence struggled with similar issues. In that room, rich with the spirit of exploration, I realized how much one's personal approach matters. And how paying attention to the particular place and the particular moment helps that style and its message to emerge.

If I presented the competitive elements like a crazed Little League dad, competition would hurt the kids, but if I "used" those competitive elements appropriately, they could help.

That thought brought me back to Hector and Felix's improv. What had I been doing there? "Using" their personal rivalry, using it as material for art.

In the theater, directors often follow that dictum. An actor will arrive for a rehearsal in tears about a love affair or the like and will be urged to "use it." The emotion can then be used to enliven a scene. It's an effective technique, first articulated by Stanislavsky.

"Using it," I realized, works in the regular classroom as well. Teachers often deal with difficult problems by integrating them into the lesson. They "use it" every day. It's a tool we all use as we work our way through moral, social, and psychological dilemmas. That, of course, was what I had been trying to say to Ms. Finney.

6.

POWER

Once the kids had worked with their bodies, senses, and feelings, they began creating characters. As the first stage of that process, I asked them to choose their favorite animal and think how it walks, talks, and eats.

Then I had them come to the front of the class one by one. Once there, they closed their eyes and took ten seconds to answer all the following questions: does your animal walk on two legs or four? Is it loud or quiet? What kind of sound does it make? Does it move quickly? Gracefully?

Next, they got into position (often on all fours) and said "Curtain" so that the audience would know that the show had begun. At that point they began walking, talking, eating, and playing, after which they went to sleep, as their animal might.

At P.S. 34 three kids chose to perform cats, but I assured them that each would be as different as three real cats. And they were. Elizabeth's cat walked with sensuous, sinewy shoulders. Monique's decided to lick herself clean after eating and before bed. And Yalmilka's reflected her own wary timidity. Other notable animals included a fine lion by Felix, a trio of dogs—two of whom were pit bulls—as well as assorted bunnies, frogs, and a superlative snake by William.

Each time a child finished, I asked the others to guess the animal. I also asked them to decide the animal's age and whether it was wild or housebroken. These distinctions not only helped the actor concentrate and deal with details, it also allowed the audience to participate.

For example, Benny did a ferocious pit bull, but when I asked him to eat three different kinds of food—hard, soft, and liquid—the audience couldn't tell the difference. But when Saul's pit bull ate, it chewed so specifically that the audience guessed right away.

When Saul finished, I emphasized how details had made the character clearer. And how we would all strive to be as detailed and specific as we could in our acting—and our writing.

Then, I asked them to take out a piece of paper and a pencil. On the board I wrote

Character Profile #1

NAME:
AGE:
FAMILY:
WISH:
FEAR:
HABITAT:

and asked the children to copy it. Once they had copied everything, I told them to think of their animal and fill in the various categories. If they had chosen a bull, I explained, the bull needed a first name. Was it Billy the Bull? Byron the Bull? Ronny the Bull? It also had to be a specific age. Was it a seventy-eight-year-old granddad? A thirty-four-year-old pop? A sixteen-year-old teenager? A baby? And who belonged in its family? I asked them to list all the other family members and their ages. Then they had to decide what the character wanted most in the world. And what it feared most ("nothing" was an unacceptable answer; everybody, I said, fears something, even if it's the fear of being thought of as cowardly). And in the last category, they described where their animal felt most comfortable. Specifically. So that they would have to say more than just "the park." If the character was a squirrel, he, Sammy the Squirrel, felt most comfortable by the grove of trees in Central Park at 79th Street and Fifth Avenue just behind the children's playground.

When we started writing, Jaime sat still. "No pencil," he said when I asked why. At my urging, Hector lent him one, but Ms. Finney heard the exchange and told Hector to take the pencil back and she called Jaime to her desk. To the rest of the class she said, "Forget excuses." Each child in her class brings a pencil every day. Without exception.

I deferred to her and went from desk to desk as the kids wrote. Here's a couple of examples.

Sue

NAME: Sue the Cat
AGE: two months
FAMILY: two brothers, six months and nine months
WISH: to scratch the couch
FEAR: brothers who yell
HABITAT: the couch. It's old and mustard colored. It has doilies.

— Monique

Lenny

NAME: Lenny the Lion
AGE: 63
FAMILY: 3 wives and 13 kids
WISH: to be king 5 more years
FEAR: hunters
HABITAT: the high grass near the watering hole in the jungle

— Felix

After the kids finished their profiles, I asked them to write a story about the animal. In the story, I explained, three things happen: the character wants something, it tries to get it, and it succeeds or fails. Here are two examples.

Greedy Bear

This character is Greedy Bear. He has ten brothers and two sisters. He is fat and short. All he thinks about is food.

One day Greedy Bear was walking and he found $50. He showed it to his brothers and sisters but he did not share it. He bought ice cream, cakes, and chips. After he ate it all, his teeth got very ugly and he never ate junk food again.

— Maria Margarita

Damaris the Bird

My character is Damaris the bird. She is a very nice bird. She is 10 years old and had a boy friend named Fred. But he died last week when a cat came into the room.

The cat jumped up and knocked the cage down. Fred flew around the room but the cat caught him, bit him, and killed him. When I came home I felt like killing that stupid black cat.

Damaris is very afraid of the cat. And she wants Fred back. She yells very loud for him.

— Kim

When the children had finished their stories and profiles, I asked them to start books. These two sections, the profile and the story, would be the first two parts of their book, I explained. The book would include animals, objects, nature, human beings, and finally a play. It also would have illustrations.

The kids loved this and asked if they could make covers and illustrate them. I said yes, and asked Ms. Finney for construction paper.

The kids drew whenever they finished an assignment ahead of the others.

❦

"I'm beginning to see how you make the transition from acting to writing," Ms. Finney said. Her tone sounded neutral, almost pleasant.

"Yes, I try to involve them as actors first," I said. "That way there's a better chance they'll respond to the writing. Good writing always begins with genuine interest," I said, wishing I hadn't added that last pontifical sentence.

"Umm," said Ms. Finney. She had apparently decided to avoid a combative posture today, and I was grateful. At first anyway. But when I explained how this emphasis on character as the first stage in dramatic writing comes from Aristotle's *Poetics*, I began to miss her penetrating questions. They stimulated me more than our discussion of sources.

"What do you think of the instructions for the story?" I asked. "Were they too generalized?"

"Well, the first words were a little difficult to grasp, but then you gave those specific examples. And I think you really made them understand how important details are."

"Yes, I realized I was talking as I might to teenagers."

"Do teenagers do animals?"

"Oh yes. And adults. I had a group at Emory University night school that did a wonderful series of animals. Otters. Elephants. Anteaters. It's a wonderful way to overcome self-consciousness. Teens, of course, are the most self-conscious, but when a few do get up in front of the class, the others often write the profiles and stories with great abandon."

"And I bet kids of all social classes respond to animals."

"Oh yes," I said, feeling as if I'd been "making nice" for hours. I wanted the old Ms. Finney back. "And farm kids, of course, choose different animals than city kids.... Are you OK, Ms. Finney?"

"Yes, why?"

"You're so...*agreeable*."

"Well, I do feel I've been a little harsh. Specialists have this way. . . ." And she stopped herself.

"What about the book?"

"Well now, that has virtues. It really does. But I wouldn't have them do the covers right away. In the first place, they're going to get tattered in their desk. And they're open, so papers will fall out."

"But how can we keep them? I need to look at them. And I can't take their whole notebooks home."

"I can get big manila envelopes. On the front they can write what they've put in and be responsible for keeping them there."

"It's like a table of contents on the envelopes."

"Exactly," she said. "And by the way, Jaime has done that pencil routine before."

"So what do you do?"

"Address the real issue."

"The real issue?"

"His writing. He's way behind and quite ashamed. We're working on his problem with concentration."

"Ah."

"You might say it's paying attention to details," she said with a devilish smile. And she was gone.

I decided to celebrate the apparent change in my relationship with Ms. Finney with a *cafe con leche* at La Taza de Azul. Soon I was sitting at my table meditating on Aristotle. According to him, everything in a play builds to its central action. But the action emerges from the needs of the characters, as do the plot and theme.

That's the problem with so much writing by kids, I decided. They watch TV and find themselves beguiled by plot, with car chases and the like.

Or "serious issues" like teen pregnancy, AIDS, and violence. Those things are important. But only under the hegemony of the characters. Real characters lead the playwright, I thought, and reminded myself to emphasize that point to Ms. Finney. "Explain why profiles come first — character's hegemony," I thought and suddenly an image from Amy's play came to me. I had worked with Amy in Atlanta five years before, but the image appeared fresh and true.

Amy's play begins with the lead character, a girl of fifteen, lying on her back looking at the stars and suddenly feeling her body burst out of its skin. Even more startling, the feeling comes as she watches the stars with her sister and her prospective stepbrothers (nice eligible boys, fifteen and sixteen). All her rage and confusion about that situation — two divorced people finding new partners and trying to meld their respective families — dwarfed the cute domestic situation. Similarly, Amy's choice, the character's bursting from her skin, changed a class assignment into art.

How many children — or adults — can write like Amy? In years of teaching I had worked with three or four. Why then did I ask every child to make art? Oh, I could teach them to follow the steps of my elaborate technique, but to what end? Wasn't I setting them up for failure? Suddenly, I felt panicky and got up to go.

As I went to pay, a large, coffee-colored woman at the register said, "Are you the new drama teacher?"

"Yes. . . . How did you know?"

"Venus — she's my daughter."

"Ah, she has such lively, beautiful eyes."

"How's she doing?" the woman asked.

"Well. Very well," I said. Now the woman smiled. She smiled much as Venus had smiled after her first answer in class. I smiled back.

She said, "My name's Carmen." I said, "I'm Daniel," and we shook hands.

Feeling better, I stood on the cold subway platform and decided to review the plays some of my less talented students had written in the past.

Two examples stood out: Maria's play about a visit to the hospital and Winnie's character profile of a cat. In Maria's play a girl visits a patient in the hospital. We discover the patient is the school secretary — hardly the stuff of great art. But when the teacher told me how Maria's parents had died of AIDS, I realized how important visits to the hospital must have been for her — what a gesture this uneventful little play was for her.

In Winnie's profile a cat snuggles up to its mother — basically a cliché. But when I learned that Winnie came to America after spending three years going from Vietnam to Thailand on a boat, and had never said anything aloud in class before, I realized how she had summoned enormous courage to create that cat character—to take charge of it, to give it life—knowing she would perform it in front of her classmates.

These two scenes would not have satisfied a large audience, but performed in the classroom, they worked, and the sense of power the writers achieved had priceless value.

Playmaking, I decided, develops an *approach*, not specific plays or solutions to problems. It teaches kids to explore. And if every child is not Amy—if he or she is unable to transform his or her feelings into riveting drama—he or she can learn how to explore feelings. And dramatize them in a credible way.

But what if those feelings get out of control, as they did the day Geneva, my other truly talented student from Atlanta, improvised a character named Jeri, a civil rights worker from Chicago. "Jeri" meets "Sandra," a local black girl, played by Cynthia, another wonderful student, and "Sandra," who understands herself much better than "Jeri," dominates the northerner and finally physically intimidates her.

The scene ended when Geneva, the actor, dissolved in tears. As we talked afterwards, it emerged that Geneva feared physical confrontation. Usually fearless as an actor, she had leaped into one of her vulnerable areas and panicked. Later, when she realized what had happened, she went back and "used" the fear.

But less talented kids might well become engulfed by their feelings. What would I do in those situations, I wondered. First, I reminded myself, I would pull back and redirect the scene. Then, I would talk with the child in private. And if it seemed appropriate I would discuss it with the classroom teacher or counselor.

Theater is *not* therapy. Working on a character as a writer or actor, we deal with feelings, but always in the context of the play or the exercise. Those activities often have therapeutic value, but that should remain secondary. And if moments ascend into art, I'm pleased. But first and foremost, the students learn how to create their worlds. The writing exercises, the books the children compile, the plays and the performances they do, all affirm who they are. They exercise that power.

7.

CONTEXT

The next session began with a whole new set of body warm-ups, which emphasized flexibility by having the kids rotate their heads, twist their torsos, move their femurs in their hip joints, and shake out their ankles and wrists. Next came sense exercises, which included building imaginary machines (another Spolin game) and a trip to the Taj Mahal.

At that point we moved on to "object characters." I asked the kids to think of an object made by human beings; it could be a Barbie doll, a dump truck, a building, but it could *not* be a rock or tree or any other part of nature—or a human being. I told them to think about how the object walked and talked.

"But mine doesn't move," said Hector.

"How would it move, if it could?" I answered. "Like if, for example, you chose a building, how would it move?"

Hector shrugged, but Kim raised her hand. "It would be big, slow, heavy," she said with absolute authority.

"Exactly. All you have to do is imagine, as Kim did. And, if I might point out, Kim, you've done it wonderfully on every assignment."

Kim's light-brown skin darkened into a blush. But for some reason I continued. "You have a superb imagination," and then, finally, "Now, who wants to be first?"

Luz, as usual, had her hand up. She also had her hair pulled back tightly in a bun. I imagined her seeing a picture of how some famous actor dressed for rehearsal and copying it. I called her up to the front.

"Go outside," I told her, "and take ten seconds for relaxation out there, then come back to the center of the 'stage area' and tell us your character's name, age, and wish, but walk and speak as your character would—not the way you would. Be the character even if a friend waves to you and calls your name or tries to make you laugh. Every move you make, every sound you utter, once you're in the room, has to be the character's."

Luz took this seriously, as she did everything related to acting. She chose a Barbie doll, a rather conventional choice—especially since I had mentioned it as an example—but her tiptoed walk and high-pitched voice melded into the quintessential Barbie.

When she had told us her name, age, and wish, I let the other kids question her and asked Luz to answer their questions 'in character.' It would be an interview.

At first the kids were shy, so I asked Luz what she was afraid of. She said, "Being left alone."

Monique picked up on my reference to the character profile and asked Luz about Barbie's habitat. Luz said, "It's supposed to be in the closet on the shelf next to Ken, but she usually throws me on the floor or leaves me outside so I'll get rained on or took."

"Who's she?" asked Kim.

"My owner," answered Luz.

"What's her name?" asked Jasmine, who seemed less shy of late. "Wendy."

"How old is she?" asked Maria Margarita.

"Eleven and a half."

I interrupted to point out that the "family" section on the profile referred to the object's owner. But that was only a brief pause in the questioning. The kids demanded answers and Luz, believing in her character, answered imaginatively. For example, Venus wanted to know why Wendy mistreated Barbie. "Because Wendy's *mami* yelled at her," Luz explained. Which prompted Hector to ask how Wendy mistreated Barbie. "Throwing me at the bottom of the closet and playing with all her other toys," came Luz's immediate response. "Weren't you listening?"

After Hector did a Cadillac and Elizabeth a comb, at least ten other kids had their hands up, but I said, "OK, take out a piece of paper and a pencil and do a profile for your object."

There was a quiet moment so I said, "Everybody remembers what a profile is, don't you?" After another pause, I said, "Take out your work on the animal and look at it. You *do* remember the envelopes and the folders you made, don't you?"

Smiles of recognition appeared and I asked Yalmilka to write the profile categories on the board. She wrote:

NAME
AGE
FAMILY
WISH
FEAR
HABITAT

and when she was done, I asked her to add another category: IMPORTANT BEING. It could be the owner, but it also could be its mother or its sister or its best friend—the somebody or something the character cares about most.

Here are some examples:

Jason

NAME: Jason the Cadillac
AGE: 6 days
FAMILY: Mr. Johnson, the boss of big business
WISH: going fast
FEAR: crash
HABITAT: the 3rd parking spot from the left in the Exxon Gas station by the bridge
IMPORTANT BEING: Carrie, the white Cadillac convertible in the next space

— Hector

Tina

NAME: Tina Tennis Shoe
AGE: 6 months
FAMILY: Connie, a 19-year-old girl
WISH: to run 1,000 miles
FEAR: being thrown out
HABITAT: a grey, cold locker
IMPORTANT BEING: Tom, her twin (the right foot)

— Kim

When the profiles were done, the kids wanted to do more interviews, but I said, "No, let's do a story about the object first. When we're done with the stories, we'll do a few more interviews. Now, in that story I want you to make the character come into *conflict* with its important being.

From the looks on the kids' faces, I knew I had to define *conflict*. "A conflict is a situation when character A wants something from character B but character B wants something else. Just the way Felix's character wanted something from Hector's character in that first improv. What did he want?"

"To go to the principal," said Felix without missing a beat.

"And I wanted to run," piped in Hector.

"So what happened between them?"

"Conflict," said Monique.

"Everybody say it: 'conflict,'" I commanded, and the whole class repeated the word.

"So it's a fight," said Felix.

"A fight is a conflict. But you can have a conflict without having a fight," I said, and cited an example from another Bronx child. That student placed a boy and girl in a McDonald's eating hamburgers. The boy wanted the girl to ask *him* out and the girl wanted him to ask *her*. They weren't fighting. But they were in conflict.

The kids seemed to understand the word *conflict*, so I set them to work. They would learn more by doing.

Bud

Hi, I'm Bud, the basketball. I live in a smelly green-walled closet. A boy named Johnathan likes to play with me. He's only 16. I'm 38. You know, I wish more than anything that I could be thrown through an NBA basketball hoop. But I'm always so scared that Johnathan will squeeze all the air out of me.

One day Johnathan tried to let the air out of me with the old air pump. But I was too smart for him. I popped out of his hands and broke the needle. Johnathan threw the old air pump on the floor and it broke.

Well, anyhow, I met the cutest little air pump. The way she pumped air into me was a dream. I wanted to go over to her house but didn't know how to ask her. Until she said she had pictures of NBA stars. When I asked if I could see them she said OK and I went. It was the best afternoon of my life.

— Kim

Sammy

Once upon a time Sammy the Building was telling his parents and his two brothers and sisters how he hated Mr. Skyscraper across the street. Mr. Skyscraper blocked all his light. And wouldn't say he was sorry.

That night he dreamed he had all new windows and could feel all the light. Then suddenly he woke up and there were people putting in all doors and windows, brand new. And not only that. Next door they were breaking down Mr. Skyscraper. Sammy was happy because he got what he wanted and that day he was one year old.

—*Jasmine*

Ms. Finney and I agreed that the interviewing game had succeeded. She was particularly pleased with Luz, whose other work had apparently been lackluster.

"Yes, she really responds to the acting," I said. "I'm just hoping it will transfer over to her writing."

"Do you have her paper there?" asked Ms. Finney. I pulled it out. We were both pleased to see that the attention Luz gave to detail in her oral responses had, in fact, reached the page.

"I was pleased with Kim," I said.

"Yes, that was clear."

"I didn't mean to embarrass her. But her imagination—it really is special."

"She comes from a mixed background. Her mother's black, dad's white. She and Mom live in the project. Dad visits," said Ms. Finney dryly.

"Does she have close friends?"

"No," said Ms. Finney, and that led to a discussion about the artist being on the outside or between worlds, as in Kim's case. It went on for about ten minutes; we both seemed to enjoy a little armchair sociology.

"Anyway," said Ms. Finney, bringing us back, "she has trouble with spelling."

That raised a touchy subject. I had not been correcting spelling on the kids' papers and now I explained why: a paper full of corrections can be discouraging; at this early stage, it's more important to inspire the kids; to teach them the joy of using the imagination; to let them feel the power of choice.

Ms. Finney said she understood that particular theory, but didn't see why it necessarily excluded learning and practicing good spelling and grammar.

"Because of time," I said. "My time is so limited. If I get into that, there will be no time for inspiration."

"Would you mind if I had the kids do spelling checks when you're not here? After you've responded to their content."

"Do *you* have time for that?"

"Not really, but I'll work it in. I want to try peer checking. It might really save time—and be a good learning tool," she suggested.

"And then they could recopy the inspired, properly spelled pages at home."

"Well, taking work home at this age in this neighborhood presents problems."

"Maybe we can tie the recopying in with the book. They can do it at odd times. And get extra credit or something. There's got to be a way."

"Hopefully," said Ms. Finney and she stood up. She started for the door in her brisk, businessperson stride, but stopped, turned around, and said, "How about if we make it a handwriting assignment, too?"

Thinking about Kim later on, I wondered why I had been so demonstrative and if it had been helpful. As Ms. Finney said, Kim was an outsider. Had I alienated her further from her peers by making her a "pet"?

It would have been so simple to pull her aside after class. I could have made the same points, given the same compliment. Why had I blurted it out like that?

Something about Kim touched me. I had been so thrilled by the authority in her voice, as she described how the building would move. It made me want to cheer for her. Which was fine. But I had overdone it. Why? That, I would have to explore on my own. It had to do with me, not her. But whatever the reason, speaking with her privately still seemed appropriate.

Later that day I tracked her down and brought her to an empty class-room. She sat on the edge of the chair at the teacher's desk in her same old jeans and grey pullover; I sat behind the teacher's desk.

"Did I embarrass you today?" I asked.

"A little."

"Sorry. But you see, Kim, you have talent—you know what that is, don't you?" Kim nodded. So I continued. "I want you to realize it. . . . Have you written before?"

"Well, I always make up stories. But I don't always write them down."

"Would you bring them in? The ones you have? I'd be happy to look at them."

"No," she said quickly.

"Well, if you ever decide you want to."

"I don't have them anymore."

"What happened?" I asked.

"They. . .I don't know."

"Well, if you ever want to talk about it or you do some more, let me know."

"I *do* want to be a writer," Kim said quickly.

"Well, we can talk about that too. Maybe at lunch next week. How does that sound?"

She nodded and I sent her back to class.

After our session, I felt better: I had expressed what I felt directly and she had heard it. What had seemed odd in the classroom had worked in the private session. The context made the difference.

Going home, I realized that I had been dealing with context all day: the interviewing game takes familiar objects and gives them a new life by imagining them with human feelings. The asking-out-on-a-date-at-McDonald's example, when we were exploring conflict, shifted the con-text and thereby expanded the meaning of conflict. And the way Ms. Finney and I had approached spelling and handwriting—that had to do with context too; we put those skills in the framework of the playwriting.

One just has to keep looking at things from different angles, I decided, as I trudged towards the subway through a February snow, feeling hopeful.

But finding those angles could be difficult, I reminded myself when I passed the ill-clad junkies who remained at their posts, waiting for deliveries next to the burned-out building. Hadn't teachers tried to find the context to excite them? To make them want to embrace and explore life? I had had a good day and solved some problems by changing contexts, but the kids lived in a world where yet another context existed: the pull of dope and money.

8.

TRANSFORMATIONS

With the third character, a part of nature, the kids not only walked and talked but also they began improvising their own scenes and learning how to write them.

Before I introduced that process, we warmed up with three exercises for communication without words that I learned from Steve Yaffe, a playwright and teacher.

In one, a group of eight to ten students stood in front of the class and, when given a signal, lined up according to height, arranging themselves without talking. That involved a good deal of gesturing and touching. Kids like Jasmine, Venus, and even Yalmilka seemed to adapt best; without words as an impediment, they seemed freer.

The second exercise, essentially a variation of the first, asked a similar group to arrange itself in color order—darkest to lightest—of shirts and blouses, again without talking. Multi-colored shirts created more than one controversy, but Clarence took charge and the second group arranged itself even faster than the first.

In the third, the remaining ten kids walked freely about the room, but as soon as one student stopped, the others had to. Ideally, the individuals in the group are so aware of each other that the students in the audience can't tell who stopped first. Saul and Benny (denizens of the infamous last row) tried to trick their teammates by stopping quickly. But after two tries, the other members in their groups got them to work as part of the team.

After each group had done all three exercises, I asked the kids to choose an element in nature. Hector asked if a rock was a part of nature. Felix said, "What do you think, dummy," but when Hector pointed out that rocks don't breathe, some of the kids began to agree with him. In the end, we voted on the issue. We decided that a rock or mountain counts because it was not manufactured by humans.

Instead of asking the kids to act right away, I assigned profiles and, after a brief reminder of what a profile was ("Look in your envelopes at the profiles for the animal and the object"), the kids wrote imaginatively. Here's a couple.

Timmy

NAME: Timmy the tornado
AGE: too old to know
FAMILY: 1 mom, 1 dad, 101 uncles, 96 aunts, 500 cousins
WISH: to destroy things
FEAR: to get weaker while destroying things
HABITAT: all over Jupiter, Mars, Venus, Saturn, and Earth
SPECIAL BEING: Lenny the lazy cloud

— Felix

Ron

NAME: Ron the rock
AGE: 12 years
FAMILY: a pebble and a boulder
WISH: to be at the base of a pine tree
FEAR: to be crushed
HABITAT: the pine tree in Massachusetts where I went to visit
SPECIAL BEING: the pine tree

—Yalmilka

Instead of having the kids write stories after the profile, I asked for a volunteer. Elizabeth had chosen a red rose, and, after she made a graceful swaying entrance and came to rest in a beautiful pose with arms above her head, she held a brief interview, in which she parried tough questions like "Why do you hurt people with your thorns?" with answers like "They ask for it."

I cut the interview short, and chose Jaime to take the part of her Special Being, Gary the Gardener.

They would now do an improv, I announced. And sent Jaime outside.

"Now, what should I tell her?" I asked the group. Nobody answered, so I said, "Think about her profile." Again there was silence. "What did she say she wished?" I finally asked.

"To grow tall and beautiful," said Maria Margarita.

"Right. And that's what she's going to try to do in this improv. Do you have any idea of how you're going to do that, Elizabeth?" She had no answer. So I opened the question to the whole class and Kim said, "By getting water and sun." "And having its bed weeded," added Monique.

"Yes, and who's going to do all that?" I asked. Almost everybody said, "Gary the Gardener," so I said, "Great. Elizabeth, or rather, Rose, you have to get him to do his job."

Before Elizabeth went out into the hall, there was a discussion about the gardener's not being able to control the sun, so it was finally agreed that there was a big tree blocking the sun, and Rose would ask Gary to cut it down.

When Jaime came in, I asked the class what he wanted. There was no profile for this character, but after a few wild answers, I asked, "What does Gary want from Rose?" Felix said, "Flowers for his girlfriend," and the improv's dynamic seemed clear to one and all.

But before Jaime and Elizabeth improvised, I said, "Take out a pencil and a fresh sheet of paper. We're going to learn how to write a play on paper. Everybody copy what I put on the board."

TIME:

PLACE:

AT RISE:

These, I explained, are the three first things you write in a play. "You decide what time the action takes place, where it happened and what the characters are doing when the play begins."

Maria Margarita asked about "AT RISE." I explained that it means "when the curtain rises." It's a holdover from the "olden days" when curtains rose instead of opening side to side. I also emphasized that we write what the audience sees at rise; e.g., MARY, who wears a black evening gown, stands, her arms folded, in the middle of her elegant living room. JOEY, who wears jeans and a torn tee shirt, is on one knee in front of her. . . .

In the current instance, the class decided the time would be noon (so the sun would be blazing down), the place would be the garden, and "at rise" Rose would be "alone on the stage stretching to get the sun that was blocked by the tree." The last stage direction before the dialogue was "Enter GARY."

I asked each child to fill in what we decided:

TIME: noon
PLACE: the garden
AT RISE: ROSE, the rose, stretches to get the sun that is
blocked by a tree. Enter GARY.

When the kids had copied everything, I pointed out that I had written the characters' names in capital letters and that they should too, that it's standard format and very helpful when a play is read aloud. Then I asked Elizabeth and Jaime to improvise. Which they did. But after a few minutes, I stopped them and asked the class to remember the first few lines Rose and Gary said to each other and select their favorites. I wrote their selections in proper dialogue form on the board.

ROSE

Cut down this tree.

GARY

Your new flowers look ready.

ROSE

And water me.

GARY

It's time to cut a few.

(GARY takes out his shears.)

ROSE

No, not me, you jerk, the tree.

I asked other kids to copy these lines, and when they were done, I pointed out that the character's name was on one line in the middle of the page and what the character said was on the next line, starting at the extreme left-hand margin.

I also explained that the stage direction, the action without words — (GARY takes out his shears.) — must be indented and enclosed in parentheses.

At that point Monique raised her hand and said that in their *Weekly Reader* the character's name was at the extreme left-hand margin followed by a colon and the speech.

I complimented Monique on her observation and agreed that book publishers often printed plays in that format, but that we would do it with each character's name on one line and the speech on the next because we would be reading them aloud later. Our format makes it easier for the actors, I said. It's also, I couldn't help adding, the way professional writers do scripts.

Once these technical points had been cleared up, I asked the kids to write the next five new lines on their own — and to do them in the proper format. Kim's next five lines were:

> GARY
> My father's favorite tree? You gotta be kidding.

> ROSE
> It won't let me grow.

> GARY
> Now just hold still.

> (GARY raises his shears.)

> ROSE
> No, don't. I'll curse your father.

> GARY
> My father?

Hiram wrote:

> GARY
> Who you callin' a jerk, you skinny, lazy weed.

> ROSE
> You don't know nuthin'.

> GARY
> At least I ain't stuck in the ground.
>
> ROSE
> And you smell bad.

For the rest of the hour, the kids worked on the scene. They wrote as many or as few lines as they wished. After these first lines, Hiram stopped writing the character's name before each speech and his conflict became one long speech. Clarence, like Hiram, had his characters trade insults. Monique's dialogue focused on how horrible it was to call people names. Kim continued to explore people's vulnerability vis-à-vis their parents and finally had her characters agree to respect one another.

The nastiness Hiram expressed in his play bothered Ms. Finney. It reflected his home life, she said. He lived with his grandmother and older brothers, and apparently the boys continually insulted one another.

"When he writes that way, he's on the way to transforming it," I said. "He didn't have a real ending today, but next time I'm going to ask him to make the characters change. Which is what action is — change. Transformation. Like we did with the names of cars."

"Wouldn't it be better to try to get him to move directly away from it?"

"I think it would be too hard a transition. This way he starts on familiar territory and then he'll step out. Also there has to be conflict in a dramatic scene, so why not start with conflicts the kids can understand."

"But why does there have to be conflict?"

I started to cite dramatic theory as developed by Freytag and Archer, but decided to tell her instead about middle-class high school kids from Dewey High in Brooklyn. "Almost all of their conflicts started as duels of insults," I said, "but then they evolved. For example, one boy, a newly arrived Russian Jewish immigrant, created a scene where a Russian teenager and an American counterpart insult each other mercilessly on the Brighton Beach boardwalk, but after the confrontation, they go for a swim and begin to respect each other as individuals. The insulting happens all the time," I said. "In a play, the boy had a chance to transform it."

"But why use it at all?"

"To change it. The kids will do it anyway, but if they learn to take it to a deeper level, they begin to work as artists: to change the culture," I heard myself saying.

"Oh, they are artists, now," said Ms. Finney, but her smile, which was actually more amused than derisive, seemed to say she accepted the point.

So I pushed on. "Issues like sex and disrespect for authority can be treated the same way. If we pretend they're not there, they simply become greater problems. But if we deal with them, if the kids explore them and try to take responsibility, we're on our way."

"To solving all our problems through art," said Ms. Finney. Her amusement seemed tinged with irritation.

"Let me tell you about a group of parents in Macon, Georgia, who squelched a play about teenage pregnancy," I said, feeling combative myself. "It was a play about a group of girls who ostracize one of their friends for getting pregnant. The parents made the kids change it to a play about a girl being ostracized for being in a mental hospital."

"That doesn't sound so terrible to me."

"It is the same point about ostracizing. But the kids felt so. . .castrated. It wasn't theirs any more."

"Because they didn't feel any power? Because their choice had been violated. Or is that an inadequate word? Would 'savaged' be better?" she said.

I couldn't help wondering about Ms. Finney. I knew she had grown up in the South Bronx, become a teacher there, married, moved to Westchester, had children, and then years later came back to the South Bronx to teach again.

But why come back? Because of the pension and the higher salary for New York City schoolteachers? Possibly. It certainly wasn't because she was a "do-gooder." She might have killed me if I accused her of that. But her tough-minded, no-nonsense talk about pensions and salaries rang false. It didn't explain why she drove so far to a dangerous neighborhood. The difference in salary and pension simply wasn't that great. And there were some suburban systems that paid much better and provided better pensions.

Maybe she did have secret "do-gooder" tendencies. Maybe it was the only job she could get at the particular moment she was applying (although with the teacher shortage now, why did she stay?). But whatever the reason, Ms. Finney chose the South Bronx. And her concern for the children was palpable. I enjoyed her constantly questioning me and my technique, because she wanted it to work. For the kids. She attacked sloppy thinking, not me personally.

Still, we had differences, I admitted as I began putting on my scarf. If I assign kids to "transform" conflict from insults and violence to constructive understanding, that might lead to "nice" plays. The issues would be raised and "resolved" according to a formula, but not necessarily dealt with.

But if the play could make an impact, if kids could touch others, get respect, approval . . . . that was what the production would do, I told myself. But if parents didn't come, as they well might not . . . . Well then it had to be for other kids and teachers. But we should do it. In a big way for the whole school.

To that end, I stopped in to see the principal, Mr. Hyman. He had always been supportive of Teachers & Writers. He listened to my proposal for a major production. He liked the idea but said the show would have to be coordinated with other auditorium commitments, particularly teacher training, and couldn't be done at night, but, if I accepted all that, it would be OK with him.

When I asked why we couldn't perform at night, he said the school was closed up tight at 4 P.M. because the neighborhood was so bad. It was too dangerous.

Wondering if Mr. Hyman was simply trying to make things easier for himself, I went to La Taza de Azul and asked Carmen if the school had ever been open at night.

"Not for a long time."

"So there are never parent meetings or school nights?"

"Yeah, there's school night. But nobody goes."

"Why not?"

"Like he said, they're afraid to go out at night."

"Are you?"

"Umhum, but that don't mean I don't want Venus to do good," she said and paused. "I never had drama when I was in school. I never had a chance like that."

I went away chastened but even more determined. We would do the play and the kids would live their transformations.

9.

STRUCTURE

Now that the kids had written scenes and created animals, objects, and elements of nature, they could work on human beings. Humans came last because kids, as soon as they are called upon to portray people, tend to portray standard TV characters. I wanted them to explore human beings as we had explored animals, objects, and nature: without "acting" images intervening. I wanted them to make their own profiles, improvs, and dramatic scenes.

As a warm-up, we played Mirrors, another classic Spolin theater game. In it, the students choose partners. One becomes the leader, and moves (in place) any way he or she feels; the other, the mirror, must imitate every move by the leader. After a few minutes, the partners exchange roles.

After watching the whole class try the game, I chose Jasmine and Deana to play it in front of everybody else. They followed each other so closely that nobody could guess who led and who mirrored. Their success encouraged them to try more difficult choices, like moving hips and arms at the same time instead of just arms. They also worked with subtle facial gestures. When they stopped, they had focused on each other so completely that they had inspired the other kids, and we were ready to work on human characters.

First, I assured the kids that they could create any type of human being—other than specific TV or movie stars: a six-month-old, a ninety-two-year-old, a teenager, a kid like themselves, a mom, a dad.

Next, I added one item to the profile: job. Maria Margarita wanted to know what job an eleven-year-old would have. I answered with "student" but afterwards wished I had elicited it from her.

Many chose kids their own age. Teenagers ranked second in popularity. But there were surprising choices as well. Monique became a fifty-year-old grandma, Jasmine a bag lady, and Saul a thirty-five-year-old cop.

Until that point Saul's written work had been unsatisfying. For example, his play format, like Hiram's, had dissolved into one long run-on sentence. So when he raised his hand to do an improv, I told him he had to copy the nature character over "in play format—with each character's name on a separate line and their speeches on lines separate from that." He sulked, but I held out and he rewrote his nature character. His improv, which he did with Hiram as his "important person" (a car thief), bristled with rage and indignation.

Clarence, perhaps inspired by Saul, volunteered to do his human being. He had chosen Michael Jordan. This presented a problem. I had forbidden movie stars, not athletes. But I really wanted Clarence—as I would any other kid—to create a character, not copy one. So I asked Clarence to make an imaginary character who played professional basketball. Clarence didn't see why, so I tried to explain.

"Michael Jordan is wonderful. But I want you to use your own imagination. Anybody can copy what's on TV. I want you to make things up. And I don't want anybody saying to you, 'Oh, Michael Jordan wouldn't do that.' I want you to be able to say, 'It's my character. I'll do it any way I want.'"

"But I did all this work," said Clarence, referring to his seven-line profile.

"I'll give you extra credit for the Michael Jordan character. But you have to do the new one."

Not pleased, Clarence returned to his seat.

While he worked on his new character, Maria Margarita did her improv. Its protagonist, an eleven-year-old girl whose important being was her best friend, found herself in a classic pre-teen friend-jealousy situation, with Monique playing the best friend. Their emotion electrified the room, but after five minutes I stopped them. Neither had given an inch; the improv clearly needed a resolution. But instead of asking the class for one, I told Maria Margarita to think about it at home. The material seemed deeply felt, the stuff of a strong play.

Luz's improv provided another exciting moment. She played a twenty-five-year-old actress. Her important person was her five-year-old daughter, played by Yalmilka. Yalmilka wanted her mother's attention and, as their improv developed, she "pitched a fit," so convincingly that Luz took the small Yalmilka in her arms and calmed her with such maternal authority that I found myself believing Luz as the "Mami" Yalmilka whimpered for.

Then Clarence did his improv. It was about a basketball player named Melvin Jones and his coach, who didn't understand Melvin. As the improv progressed, it became clear that Melvin's rage reflected more of Clarence than of Michael Jordan. I was enormously pleased.

At that point I told everybody to take a clean sheet of paper and to write a scene in which the human character comes into conflict with his or her important being, and to use proper play script form, starting with TIME, PLACE, and AT RISE.

There was some confusion, but I reminded them they had a copy of proper play script form in their envelopes. "It's all there in your Nature Scene," I said.

The kids struggled, so I went from child to child, reminding them to have the speaker's name on a separate line, to indent and add parentheses with stage directions, to remember that conflict demanded that a wanting must confront another wanting. And when possible, to try to make the conflict transform into cooperation or understanding.

Saul, now inspired, did his format well and built the same wonderful conflict that had emerged in his improv. When I read what he had written, I asked him to see if the cop and crook could come to an understanding. Saul didn't believe his characters would. Nor was he, Saul, interested in a happy ending. He wanted to tell the story his way. So I deferred. And it turned out to be a good, tough *film noir* scene with a killing at the end.

The other kids had varying success with their human scenes. What Luz wrote didn't measure up to her improv. Maria Margarita's seemed to broaden and deepen the conflict in hers. Kim, who hadn't done an improv, built a harrowing conflict between a father and daughter. Jaime still struggled with structure. Venus worked slowly.

"I'm a little mystified by your priorities," said Ms. Finney. "You don't worry about spelling, but you're merciless with a boy like Clarence, who's expressing a perfectly normal bit of hero worship."

"I have nothing against hero worship. But it's very important that Clarence create his own character."

"Yes, yes, you've said that, but aren't you restricting his 'choice', his 'sense of power' with this. . .I almost said 'censorship,' " said Ms. Finney, pulling back from her Jesuit-sharp logic.

Ms. Finney and I smiled at each other, so I felt free to say, "It's a good thing you don't go in for hyperbole, Ms. Finney."

"I guess I'm worried about Clarence," she said seriously. "This is one of the few times I've seen him volunteer, to express interest. I really thought you were squelching it."

"But he did it. And he got to his feelings about his coach."

"You could have lost him," she said, responding to my cavalier tone.

"And Saul, too," I said. "I assumed they would be capable and willing. If they would have quit or failed, I would have tried to see them individually," and I began telling her about Enrique.

Enrique, a slow student at another South Bronx school, lived alone with his sixty-year-old grandmother and seemed to crave contact and attention from me or any other adult. He interrupted. He pouted. He refused. He attacked other kids. Anything to keep me from teaching the rest of the class. At first, I took time from the rest of the class, but the extra attention only fed his voracious need—and irritated the other kids. So I began treating him like the others in class and even made him leave on occasion. But I also arranged to see him during my free period on a regular basis and told him I would have less time for our free periods if he wasted time in class. He never became a perfect student, but he did finally write and perform a play.

Ms. Finney shot me a roguish smile. "You bribed him."

"I prefer to think of it as creating structure," I said, smiling but feeling a bit shaky. "It's the same as saying we're going to do animals first, objects second, nature third, and humans fourth. I give a structure. They are creative and have choice—power—within the structure," I said.

Interested but not completely satisfied, Ms. Finney said, "Yes, I like that order for the characters, especially that the animals come first. The animals speak so clearly to kids at this age."

"And now they're ready for the human beings," I said, and then, hearing a bit of self-righteousness in my tone, added, "I just hope it's clear in the writing too," tapping the papers in my manila envelope.

After a pause Ms. Finney said, "You know what I don't understand? I just don't see why you couldn't limit the fancy cars and pop songs the way you limit movie stars and athletes. Could personal preference play any part in that?" And off she went, clicking high heels.

What a mess of contradictions, I thought. I pretend to have an approach — this choice-power business — but, as Ms. Finney points out, I subvert it by my authoritarian "limits" or structure. The rhetoric sounds good. But the message the kids get is "no sports stars, no movie stars." Why *can't* they be "transformed" the way I have the kids "transform" cars and pop songs in the sense exercises?

And what about Saul's point? Does there always have to be a transformation? What if a character is, in fact, incorrigible? Can't he die, as he does in Saul's scene? Why should my optimistic sensibility rule? If I really believe in the kids' saying what they feel, how can I object to Saul's saying what he feels? The act of his writing is the message. Maybe he'll turn out to be another Ayn Rand. Or grow up to feel art is frivolous. But that would be who he is. His writing does not exist to make me feel "nice."

Ms. Finney had really tapped a vein of self-doubt this time. I went home quite upset.

On the subway, I thought about Mike, a Mexican-American boy. Working with Mike was my first teaching experience. It was the spring of 1964 and I, a senior at the University of California, Santa Barbara, had organized a tutoring program at the local junior high school. I paired what are now called "at risk" high school students with volunteers from the university. Mike became my partner. At first, I worked with him at the school, but then he got suspended for an infraction of the rules. His father was a construction worker and, coincidentally, had a job at the university. So we arranged for Mike to ride to work with him and have tutoring sessions with me on campus. Mike came to the first couple of sessions, but then started hanging out with the surfers on the nearby beach. He and I had several talks, and after them he would come for a session or two, only to disappear again. I also talked to his folks. Nothing changed, except my mood. I felt I had failed.

And then I went to a civil rights lecture where a young black man, probably no older than I, spoke about his experiences in the South. He said many interesting and inspiring things, but one in particular stuck with me: "You can't let the Man get your mind." By that he meant you can't allow yourself to be deterred by the logic of, say, a sheriff's proclamation that demonstrations could lead to violence. There is, of course, a certain validity in that point of view, but if you believe in what you are doing, you adhere to your own logic. So in this case, you would say, "Yes, there are dangers in demonstrations, but the dangers of not demonstrating are far greater."

After the lecture, I asked the young man about my problem with Mike. And this preacher of non-violence said, "I would tar his butt."

Later it became clear to me that the Man—in this case the Good Liberal Man—had my mind. I had refused to do what I really wanted to do: to read the riot act to Mike, to set my limits, and say "If you don't show up, I will call the school authorities." And if that violated my ideas of "not being a bully" and "helping him in a new way," well, I had to do it anyway.

The next time I spoke with Mike, I told him how he was ruining his chance and hurting his family, and that he had caused me a lot of trouble. If he didn't show up, I would call the school and have him placed on the truant list. That became the limit, the structure. After that, Mike showed up. And we worked.

If I could have put Mike into an ideal world, he might have come around on his own. But he lived in his world, and I in mine. What I finally gave him was myself. And in my role as authority, I had my limits. I became a factor in the equation. And if he felt I had my rigidities, at least they were clear. He knew he was dealing with me.

Thinking about the Bronx kids again, I decided to reaffirm my personal limits—no movie stars or athletes, etc. If we wanted to build human characters that worked in the limited time we had, *I* needed those limits. I also would keep looking for other ways, ways that would allow me to drop the restrictions. But in the meantime, we would work within my limits.

TECHNIQUE

After my meditation about rigidity, I felt particularly good about the next lesson: writing monologues. It allowed the kids to broaden and deepen their characters, to find their respective voices — thereby moving from clichés and stock types to the special and compelling.

After a simple yoga breathing exercise and general stretching warm-up, I presented the notion of monologue.

"That's stupid. Who's he gonna be talking to?" said Felix. He was referring to his seventeen-year-old street kid character.

"The audience," said a long-suffering Hector. He looked spiffy in a white sweatsuit with a designer label.

"So how come he ain't talkin' to the 'audience' in my scene?" Felix wanted to know.

"Think of it this way," I said, ever anxious about the smoldering antagonism between Felix and Hector, "your scene has ended and your character is alone. He can be on the street. Or left alone in the room. Or in bed that night. But he is thinking about what happened. And gets to say all the things he feels but might not say to the person. It could be 'I love you.' Or 'I hate you' or 'Your breath smells' or whatever. And after he's finished exploring the secret thoughts, he can tell his mom or sister or dad. Or anybody else. It's time for your characters to speak from the heart. And when they've said it all, they can decide what to do."

"What if my character ain't afraid of nuthin'?" asked Saul.

"Well, maybe he's not afraid of crooks, but how does he feel when his mother's crying?" I asked, and Saul seemed to get it.

"What do you mean 'decide what to do'?" asked Kim.

"Well, your character just had a scene with his or her important being. They've separated — gone different ways. And then your character says all he or she wants to say. So then what? Is your character going to go after his or her important being to apologize? Is he or she going to pick a fight? Run away? I don't care what, but the character has to decide to *do* something.

"Now don't forget to write the TIME and the PLACE and to indicate what's happening AT RISE," I said, and the kids began.

Kim picked up her pencil and started to write the following monologue.

TIME: Saturday at 2:00
PLACE: the kitchen
AT RISE: MOM has just gone out.

DENISE

Why can't you listen? You say you want to talk. You sit me down and say "Let's talk," but you never listen. All you care about is him. I'm just his daughter to you. You don't love me. You don't even care about me. Except to get him here. And when he gets here, he's so mean. I hate him. I don't care what you say. I hate him. I never want to see him again. I won't stay in the house with him. If he comes here, I'm going to run away.

Yalmilka, who had become more interested in the character she did for Luz—the five-year-old who 'pitched a fit'—asked if she could write about her. I said, "Sure. But do me a profile before you go into the monologue." Here's what she wrote:

TIME: 8 A.M.
PLACE: MARIA's bedroom
AT RISE: MARIA sits alone on her bed.

MARIA

Mami, you put your arms around me and I feel so good and then you go. Why do you have to go? Why can't I come with you? I hate the old nurse. She's stupid. And fat. And ugly. I hope she won't come in here. I don't want her in here. If she tries to come in here I'm going to lock the door.

(She locks the door.)

There was anger in many of the other monologues as well. Sensing another opportunity for transformation, I decided to take the exercise a step further—to do improvs based on the monologues.

Monique went first. In her monologue the grandmother character complained about young people. It was excellent, but the grandmother's action invited a response. When Monique finished, I asked her who else she would like to overhear the conversation. "God," she said (possibly facetiously, but I took it seriously). So I asked Saul to play God, and they improvised a funny scene that developed into God's complaining about all the complaints!

Elizabeth's monologue dealt with friendship and betrayal among teenagers. When I asked what character she wanted to overhear her monologue, she said Jennifer, the friend who had left. Jennifer, she explained, had come back for her umbrella and heard everything that Monica had said. The monologue that followed turned into a really angry fight.

Other scenes brought in sympathetic grandparents, moms and dads, little sisters, teddy bears, Barbie dolls, etc.

"You can do all this — and you do it well," said Ms. Finney. "But I could never do it."

"Why not?"

"Why not? I just don't think like that. You have to have a special point of view. An 'artistic' point of view," she said, biting off the word.

"No, the kids do it all. All you have to do is listen. It was Monique who chose God to listen to the grandmother's monologue. This girl who I had previously thought of as an intelligent but unimaginative child."

"But you chose Saul to play God."

"You would have too. If you know the kids, your instincts tell you which way to go."

Ms. Finney allowed that she might have, but she might also have chosen Clarence, and we proceeded to discuss listening as a dying art. We agreed people simply don't pay attention any more. Was TV to blame? Or drugs? Or maybe the deterioration of family? We couldn't decide.

Coming back to the lesson, I said, "The thing I'm a little worried about is the simplistic quality of the monologues. I wish the kids would give more details. Not just say 'I hate you' but say why and how."

"That would become too 'intellectual,'" said Ms. Finney.

"*Touché.* But I meant that the really interesting stuff comes out in the details. Like when Clarence started going on about the coach picking on him," I said, and when Ms. Finney seemed interested, I gave her another example, a monologue by Karen, a thirteen-year-old girl from Coney Island.

Karen's monologue came from a sick old woman in a hospital. Karen tried to write about the woman's loneliness, and as an attempt to set time as well as place, she had a sixties-style peace march going on outside. In the character's mind it seemed like a war. And that feeling eclipsed the loneliness. After reading the monologue and discussing the situation with Karen, I recommended that Karen write about the peace march — as a way to explore her parents and their generation. The detail revealed a whole other vein of interest.

"Yes, but just remember they're fifth graders," said Ms. Finney.

Thinking back over my experience, I became more sympathetic to Ms. Finney's anxiety. I had started teaching children to write plays in 1985. Until then, I had always taught drama as Creative Dramatics or scene study. And for many years I hadn't taught at all. What made me feel kids could write a play?

As I tried to recall my reasoning those first weeks in Macon, Georgia, where I had gone to do a stint as an artist-in-residence, I realized that the vision, the hope of kids writing plays, had emerged as a negotiating point.

The school and community leaders wanted me to form a children's theater. As an artist-in-residence, I was, in fact, contractually bound to work one day a week in the community. Usually, however, that meant a night class in acting for adults. But the school and community leaders were insistent. The community needed a children's theater.

"What is so important about a children's theater?" I asked a painting contractor who served as my liaison to the community. He explained that Macon's economy traditionally had depended on its cotton mills and manufacturing, but with the cheaper mills in Hong Kong, Korea, and Taiwan, most had gone out of business. Macon needed to attract new industries. But each time a manufacturer was interested, a company executive would eventually ask about the "cultural resources" available to the children of the executives who might move to Macon. At that point, the resources were slim; a children's theater would strengthen them enormously. Also, the Macon Little Theatre, which did adult plays in the wealthy north part of town, had undermined the last two groups who tried to do adult plays. It also chose conservative plays (censoring even these) and only used its favorite actors. Some people in town wanted a theater for adults and others wanted one for children. But they needed somebody with theater experience to put everything together. I fit that role.

His logic was irrefutable, but I felt bullied. So I decided to set my own conditions. I would do the organizing if I could experiment with the children doing all the writing. The school and community people thought there might be room for such a program at some point, but I insisted on doing our first production that way. I also said the first production had to come after training—that it was a bad precedent to do theater without training. The leaders agreed, still thinking, I believe, that they would finally end up doing *Oliver* or the like once the program of summer workshops had been organized and the pressures of a production were upon us.

But at that point I was committed to the children writing. And, even if I questioned my ability to stimulate the kids and wondered if they could actually do it, I was determined. They would write not only the play but also the music, and they would choreograph the dancing.

The show turned out to be an extraordinary success. The kids' work emerged as a vital new force in the community. It not only entertained, it also made the children's concerns important to the community. People filled the house every night, they wrote letters to the editor of the paper, they got the newspaper and the three TV stations to review it. The reviewers sang our praises. The kids felt good about themselves. They began to sense their own power.

This success made me realize I had found a calling. But what did that do for Ms. Finney? She certainly wasn't going to stop teaching to form a children's theater—just so she could teach playwriting. It was my job to teach the techniques, so that she could learn to teach them. Was I doing this? Or was I building a "cult of personality"?

This question seemed to demand a *cafe con leche*, so I went off to La Taza de Azul, barely noticing the junkies as I passed them.

As I sipped the steaming coffee, I reviewed teacher-training courses I had given. They had been of two types: inspiration/exposure and hands-on supervision.

The inspiration/exposure courses worked extraordinarily well. One, given as a part of a Teachers & Writers enrichment program in New York City's District 5 (Harlem), became a top draw after school on Friday afternoons. It offered the teachers a chance to socialize with each other as well as an opportunity to explore writing with professional writers. Five different writers taught. Each of us offered an introduction to our respective specialties. When the series of Friday afternoons ended, the teachers had sampled poetry, short fiction, novels, science writing, and plays.

Another introduction/exposure course, this one in Macon, opened up a series of spirited discussions: should children be allowed to write about drugs and pregnancy and sex? What role should specialists play in a class-room? How much time should be spent on grammar and spelling? There seemed to be a real interest in exploring these everyday problems with other professionals.

But neither of these workshops — nor any other short-term exposures — prepared the teachers to do a full playwriting and production course. They simply introduced the teachers to an approach, offered a few exer-cises, and made the teachers aware of books like Spolin's. They showed the teachers it was possible.

In a course sponsored by the Dramatists Guild (the professional playwrights' organization), a week of inspiration/exposure was combined with nine weeks of follow-up visits to the teacher's classroom and small group discussions among teachers trying out various techniques. That combination proved quite effective.

Still, Ms. Finney and I lived the ideal. She saw everything I did. She worked alongside me. She influenced me — taught me — and tried out her own ideas with me. There was room for give-and-take.

Ms. Finney's remark about lacking an "artistic point of view" came to mind and I began to smile. Good teachers like Ms. Finney *are* artists — they just don't know it.

My real concern should be my work teaching playwriting. I began to review the previous lessons. Had I emphasized the main object — elicting impulses from the kids? Had I shown how the teacher went from improv to writing, emphasizing the writing a bit more in each lesson? It seemed to me as though I had. But questions remained: why didn't I ask Ms. Finney to explain why she might have chosen Clarence over Saul to play God? Had I explained how the work makes the kids feel better about themselves? Should I organize a training session for the other teachers at P.S. 34?

BAFFLING MOMENTS

Feeling good about the extra session on character and especially good about the wonderful new improv set-up that emerged from it, I told the kids that, after a good yoga stretch and a short sensory awareness trip to the Brazilian rain forest, they would be ready to start writing a play.

"What have we been doing?" said Jaime, whose work had been improving, particularly since we started on the human character. His human character, based on his big brother, fascinated him.

"Well, these have been exercises," I said. "You've learned how to explore characters and how to lay out a play on a page. And some of you may choose to write about your characters—human or otherwise. But I do have one requirement."

"It's gotta be about Snow White." Amazingly, this comment came from Maria Margarita. If anybody would have chosen to imitate *Snow White*, to do something correct and proper, it would have been she. That day she had put on jeans and a sweat shirt—the ultimate concession—and now she clearly felt I was stopping her from writing her friendship-betrayal play.

"No. I want you to choose a topic you're curious about—something you do *not* understand. For example, you're walking down the street, your best friend walks by and you don't say hello. You're not angry at her. She hasn't done anything. You just don't say hello. And you don't know why. Which bothers you. That is worth writing about. But if your best friend had, in fact, been dating your boyfriend, then snubbing her would be understandable and not worth writing about. Or if you didn't care that you were behaving oddly, if you just walked by and didn't wonder and worry about it, that wouldn't be worth writing about either. We write plays to discover what we feel. Now, can anybody think of an incident where you did something you don't understand—and it bothered you?" I asked, hoping some examples would clarify this concept.

After a few moments of gentle prodding, I said, "Kim, what about you?" Without missing a beat she said, "My aunt offered to take me to the country and as soon as she asked I said no. I didn't think or anything. I just said no. And I wanted to go. I just . . . ." She broke off. It was a perfect example, but before I could wax eloquent about Kim's creativity, Clarence raised his hand and described a game where the coach said, "Don't shoot. We're ahead. You should just pass and dribble till time runs out." But Clarence shot. And his humiliation, rage, and confusion still reverberated in the room.

Yalmilka said she had wanted new shoes and had pestered her mother till she got them, but once home, Yalmilka let them sit in the closet. I asked if they hurt her feet, and she said, "No." With curt defiance.

At that point I asked everybody to take a piece of paper and a pencil and think of an incident in which they did something they did not understand—and were still bothered by it, still curious about it. Once they had decided what it was, I asked them to describe it in prose. "I want all the details," I said. "Where were you? What were you wearing? Who else was there? What were they wearing? Was it hot? Or cold? Was it inside or out? Was there any scent? And how did you feel? Were you sad? Or angry? Or confused? Write it all down in about a page."

Many of the children started, but others were paralyzed. I went to Elizabeth, whose graceful body was contorted into a Chinese puzzle, and asked her if there were anything about her family she didn't understand. Elizabeth allowed that she didn't understand her father or her feelings about him. I told her to think of one moment when she felt particularly confused and describe it.

Hector said he understood his family perfectly—and everything else as well. So I asked him if he ever saw anything on the street he didn't understand, and he mentioned a bag lady he had fought with. I suggested he write about the fight.

Hiram claimed he understood everything he saw on the street, as well as his family and the rest of his life, so I suggested that he write one of his dreams (writing about dreams would be the next phase of the work, but I hoped he might respond to it more readily than a "real" incident). He sat a moment and then grabbed his pencil. I made a mental note to have him come back to the first part of the assignment when the others moved on to dreams.

Jasmine understood everything, and didn't dream, so I suggested she write a "What if" incident as an alternative. "What if an angel came down from heaven and granted you one wish?" I asked. "Write what would happen." Jasmine, who had felt bedeviled by the original assignment and expressed it with a tight, drawn look on her lovely face, let go of the tension. Her face was even prettier as she worked on the "angel" assignment.

Finally everybody was working.

Anna, who had been absent often, that day seemed open and responsive in her bright orange sweatsuit. She wrote:

> I was in the park with my new bike. It was a hot day. Everybody was sweating but I was cool on my bike. Carmen, she was wearing a turquoise tank top and white shorts, asked if she could borrow my bike. I said yes but I really felt no. When she brought it back there was a scrape on the fender. I saw it but I didn't say anything.

I asked Anna if she and Carmen were friends. "Best friends," she answered.

Victor wrote about sneaking into a public pool the previous summer:

> I jumped in. Paulie was sitting on the side. His stomach was fat and sloppy. I pulled him in and stuck his head in the water. I knew I was holding it too long but I kept doing it till I almost drowned him.

As the kids finished writing about things they did not understand, I spoke to them individually about things they had seen.

On a typical day they saw drug dealers, prostitutes, and fights, but, as dramatic as those characters and incidents may appear to many of us, the kids found them prosaic. When I asked Monique, for example, about things she had seen and the issue of drug dealers came up, she said she knew exactly how to handle them: don't look when you walk by their door and they'll be nice to you on the street. To her, drug dealers were a bit like eccentric old folks or a barking dog; they were part of life and you learned how to protect yourself from them. You didn't reason why. On the other hand, Monique didn't understand why her big sister always cried in the movies, even when the film seemed so happy.

Tyrone, who continued to wear neatly pressed pants, told me he couldn't understand how a white girl he saw in the park could be so disrespectful to her grandmother. A parent yes. Not a grandparent.

One by one the rest of the kids finished a personal incident and began ones they had seen and remained confused by. Near the end of the

hour a couple of kids had finished the observed images, so I decided to add an assignment: "By next week you should all write three images you do not understand:
   — Something that happened to you
   — Something you saw or heard
   — Something you dreamed."

The introduction of dreams caused a big stir. Almost all the kids remembered dream images. They were also fascinated by their dreams and could remember them in exquisite detail. Only Saul and Clarence claimed they never dreamed, so I asked them to wait after class (lunch was the next period). I told the others they could work on them at their own speed at home.

Sitting alone with me, Clarence allowed that he had daydreams, images that came to him in a half-dream state, like stealing a pass and dribbling to the opposite basket, doing a reverse layup, and just hanging in mid-air.

Saul assured me he never even daydreamed, so I asked him to imagine what he wanted most in the world, to describe it and tell me how he got it. He wanted an Uzi submachine gun, and described going into a gun store and slapping a $1000 bill on the counter. I smothered my moral objections to his choice and urged him to give realistic details. Was the counter glass? What was in it? Which pistols?

Ms. Finney was fascinated by the change in Maria Margarita's attitude. "She always does her work, but with a certain vehemence—'See I did it, what are you gonna do now?'—but this playwriting she really wants to do for itself."

"Did you hear her question about *Snow White?*" I said. "It was as if I were taking her new friend away."

"Another betrayal," said Ms. Finney.

I didn't have anything to add to that, but said feebly, "Maybe this will be a turning point. Maybe she'll learn to trust."

"Yes, in the safe, secure world of show business."

"I'm not advocating that these kids go into show business. I want them to learn to enjoy art and to make artistic decisions," I said rather hotly.

"Yes, that was cheap," said Ms. Finney, and after a moment she asked how I felt about Saul and his Uzi machine gun.

"I've had pleasanter moments," I said. "But I had a hunch it might transform...."

"Ah yes, the old transformation gambit."

"Actually, I've thought that through a little further and I've remembered a perfect example," I said, feeling ready to do battle. "Two years ago I taught a Brooklyn junior high girl, who chose to do a prostitute character. We were doing the interviewing game and she gave snotty-tough answers to a number of snotty-tough questions. But after class she asked if her character could change and become a businesswoman in the next phase of the work. I said that would be fine—very professionally, not betraying my pleasure. And asked her to explore how and why the character changes."

"OK. So?" asked Ms. Finney.

"So I allowed her to explore what she wanted. If I would have censored her—"

"As you did Clarence."

"You're full of cheap shots today," I said quickly.

"No. He could have been Michael Jordan."

"But I told you I have my limits," I said, referring to a conversation we had after I came to my conclusions about my personal limits.

"Yes, but I still think that's having it both ways."

"It's what I can do," I said.

"I hope you're as 'understanding' of them as you are of yourself, when they don't turn in their homework," said Ms. Finney.

Alone, I searched around for a snappy rejoinder until I realized I had become quite angry. I felt as if Ms. Finney had not pointed out things, she was only finding fault. She also had belittled serious examples. Maybe I did tell long stories, but there was always a point.

I also wished I had explained my rationale for starting with baffling moments. Ms. Finney should know why, especially since we had talked. And what about crediting Conrad Bromberg, my playwriting teacher.

The writing aspect of Playmaking derives directly from his approach. She wouldn't even let me. . . .

What was going on here? Was I teaching a technique or impressing Ms. Finney? Who was she anyway? The Great Teacher Authority, who would legitimize my work? My mother? An attractive woman I wanted to impress?

There were probably elements of all that. But after I said hi to Carmen, ordered my *cafe con leche*, and settled into my seat at La Taza de Azul, I still wanted to tell Ms. Finney that this technique gets the children to focus on characters and personal feelings, not plot. And that focusing on character and personal feelings allows the kids to explore themselves.

"Relax," said Carmen, when she brought the coffee. "Those kids—they're monsters sometimes."

"It's not the kids. It's the teachers."

"Ms. Finney—she's all right," Carmen said.

"Well . . .," I said.

Carmen looked at me and off she went.

"Ummm," I said, taking her exit as a comment and settling back to lick my wounds and to focus on combining playwriting with other disciplines.

As I thought about other ways of combining disciplines, I remembered a playwriting and history session I did in Gwinnet County, Georgia, an oral history project I did in Harlem, and a Drama and Social Issues course I taught in Atlanta.

The history project covered explorers and early settlements in the U.S. In approaching that period, I asked the children, sixth graders at a white middle-class school, the same questions I asked the group at P.S. 34: "What don't you understand? And of what you don't understand, what do you really care about?" Each kid wrote. Then, because of time requirements, I chose five of them. I asked the other children to choose one of the five selected topics. Groups developed from those choices. Within each group, the children chose characters and, after some struggling with the technique of improvisation, began developing plays. Which led to written scenes. And finally readings. All in ten sessions!

The oral history project, an experiment initiated by Teachers & Writers, combined anthropology and writing. The students, fourth graders in Harlem, interviewed older people and explored the neighborhood from different angles, e.g., drawing maps and looking at old slides. Next I asked the kids the crucial questions: "What don't you understand? And do you really care about that?" Then they began to work imaginatively by writing about baffling moments, developing characters, doing improvs, and finally creating dramatic structure and writing plays.

I taught a drama and social issues class at a private high school in Atlanta. The students were quite bright and analytical, so there was a lot of discussion. But as soon as I asked them to focus on incidents and characters they did not understand, the class became galvanized. The kids broke up into two groups and chose characters to develop. Then through improvisation and group writing they developed a text that they performed with great success as lunch-time theater.

At that point I looked up and Carmen asked, "You want to try something?"

"What?" I said.

She handed me a dish of *flan*.

12.

FOCUSING

At the next session, we started with yoga breathing, did a hang-out, and finished the warm-up with the second part of our trip to the rain forest. Then I asked the kids which of their three baffling moments they cared about most.

"I care about my character most," said Maria Margarita, her anger barely below the surface, and others murmured assent.

"Well, as I said, there may be a way to combine your character with your baffling moments."

"But one's about my dad, the other's about my friend."

"Isn't there another character in each of those?"

"Me?"

"A character *based* on you. You never said those things. You imagined a character saying them. Just as you imagined a character like your father and one like your friend. Right?"

"Yes," said Maria Margarita tentatively.

"Well, why not put all three of them in the same play? Maybe she's having trouble with her friend because of pressure from her Dad . . . ."

I was afraid I might have given too much direction, so I quickly said, "Or maybe they can meet another way. You think of something. You're the writer."

The kids seemed unsure. "For example, if I were doing this exercise, I might write a scene in which a character based on me teaches a class and another where a character based on me has a fight with his wife at home. I could make them parts of the same play with one scene in the classroom and another at home," I said and waited.

Felix asked, "Do you got kids?"

"No, in fact, I don't even have a wife any more. I was making that up."

The kids seemed to be digesting the biographical data until I said, "But you don't have to use your human characters. We can make all new ones now. Or you can use your animal or your object. It's up to you."

"You mean make my basketball shoes a character in the play?" Clarence asked. I couldn't help noticing that Clarence wore a new pair of sneakers that day.

"Or your tornado or your bison. Just as long as the work we're going to do today begins with your baffling moment."

"What do you mean by 'begins'?" asked Kim.

"That's exactly the question I wanted," I said. Maria Margarita and Monique exchanged glances. Had I been favoring Kim?

"Once you've selected your moment, I want you to choose two characters that come from it or are suggested by it and do profiles of them. If you're using a character you've already done a profile of, great. You can start on the next step: 'a day-in-the-life.'

"A day-in-the-life tells what happens to a character in a typical day. But not a general story like 'He got up and went to school, came home and watched TV until bed.' I want you to give me details. 'He woke up, shuffled barefoot to the bathroom, took off his green and white striped pajamas, leaving them in a pile on the floor while he took his cold shower. For breakfast, he had Froot Loops and orange juice.' You see, the details tell us about the person. What kind of a person wears green and white striped pajamas but no slippers and leaves his pajamas on the floor? What kind of person eats Froot Loops? Is he different from somebody who has a doughnut and coffee and sleeps in the nude? He is, isn't he? The choices people make tell us about them. Now, who can tell me a detail about somebody's clothes that tells us about that person?"

Kim raised her hand and said, "If somebody wears bell bottoms, they're living in the sixties."

I took a quick look at my pants. Fortunately mine didn't flare at the bottom—that day. "Yes, that's a wonderful example," I said purposefully, and again noticed a look from Maria Margarita to Monique. "What about books people read? For example, who reads *Batman*?"

"Everybody," said Felix.

"I don't. Ms. Finney doesn't. What does that say about us?"

"You ain't chilly," pronounced Felix.

"Good. Then telling what we read says something about us. Just as the food we eat and the clothes we wear and what we say and do."

"Now, one last thing: I want you to give these characters fictional names. Even if you are going to describe what you might do or what your mother might do, the character is not you or your mother. It is, as I said before, based on you or your mother. So, your character, Kim, she's based on you, but later when you're writing the play you might want her to do something you've never done. If she's named Kim, you might say 'I've never done that, or I would never do that,' but if, say, she's 'Fran' she can do what she wants. OK?"

Kim nodded and I looked at Maria Margarita.

"Right, Maria Margarita?" I said. She shrugged.

"You can choose something that reminds you of the person it's based on. So you might choose a name like Anna Angelita."

She nodded politely.

"Try it this way. You'll see how much fun it is. OK, let's write."

As I circulated, I found some of the kids, who had begun their days-in-the-life, rushing ahead to the day at school or on the job, and urged them first to tell me about breakfast. Jaime said his character didn't eat breakfast. "Good," I said. "That tells us something about him. Write it down. 'He skipped breakfast—as he usually did.'"

Luz, who was writing a wonderfully detailed account of a young girl dressing for school, said her character usually didn't eat breakfast, but that day she would because she wanted to please her mother. "Great," I said, "write all that down. It tells us how she feels about her mother."

When I asked Felix for more details about school, he said, "If I put it all down, I'd be here all day."

"No," I said, "choose the important things. But describe those well. For example, if he asks a girl out, I want to know where she was standing when he went up to her, what she was wearing, who else was around. All of that tells us about him."

The kids started well enough, but quickly lapsed into generalizations, especially when the characters came home. So I said, "It's OK to have your character watch TV but it's not OK for you to stop there. You have to say he watched re-runs of 'Cheers,' lying on the floor with his yellow cat, Jacob, or he watched the Yankees with a scorecard that he marked on every pitch and anything Don Mattingly did with a special red pen. . . . Details, folks, details."

The kids wrote. Elizabeth finished first, but when I looked at her paper I saw melodramatic events, Elizabeth's notion of what a play should be about. "Was this a typical day?" I asked.

"No, this is the day the play happens," said Elizabeth.

"Well, it's terrific. But you're a little ahead of the rest of us. Tell you what: let's save this paper. You'll use it later. But right now, I'd like you to write a typical day, what usually happens to her."

"But why?"

"Because you have to know her regular life first. It may give you ideas for other actions, ones you never thought of."

Elizabeth reluctantly took out a fresh sheet of paper, but eventually settled down to write about her favorite old slippers, about waiting for the bathroom because of her brother. . . .

As others finished, I told them to write the day-in-the-life of the other main character. Some got deeply into this other day-in-the-life, others barely started. At the end of the period, I told the kids they should finish the two days-in-the-life before the next session, when we would start writing the play itself.

That session began with a repeat of the hands-laced breathing exercise I taught the first day and a quick game of Statues. About three quarters of the kids had finished both days-in-the-life. I decided to compromise. I would let the other kids finish theirs. The three-quarters who finished, I asked to add a single sentence to each paper. "Tell me what these characters want from the other. The one thing they want most," I said.

"What?" exclaimed Hector.

"If you've written a whole day-in-the-life, you know a lot about both of these characters. Think about what they really want from each other. Is it love? Or money? Or encouragement? But choose only one. The most important one."

As the kids finished this last part of the day-in-the-life, I asked them to draw pictures of the characters until everybody else had finished. When they had, I told them to take a fresh sheet of paper and to start writing.

"Just like that?" said Venus.

"As long as it's in proper play form."

"Proper play form?" asked Felix.

"The way we did the play about your part of nature and your human character. Look in your envelope."

The kids opened their envelopes and looked at proper play form. They also got out fresh sheets of paper. But few began writing. Finally, Monique articulated what bothered many of them: "I don't know where I'm going. . . ."

"Yeah," cried Jaime, "I don't know what's gonna happen." Others murmured their agreement.

"Well," I said slowly, "if you knew, I'd be disappointed," and paused. The kids waited, intent. "You see, it's very, very important that you *don't* know. Just as I *don't* want you to understand the baffling moments you wrote about."

"But this is the story," said Maria Margarita.

"And whose story is it?"

"Mine," said Maria Margarita.

"Yes. But who else's?"

Maria Margarita and the others waited.

"Who does the action?"

"The characters," said Kim.

"Right," I said emphatically. "Good writers listen to their characters. You have to let them act—do things. That's what will make your work come alive: your characters listening to each other, reacting to each other. If you plan too much ahead, you'll be pushing them around. And they'll be puppets, not characters. So start with the first line and let the characters lead. They'll take you back to your baffling moment and help you to understand it. It's going to be a long road, but you'll get there—if you set them free. Don't worry about the story, the plot. It will come in its own good time."

"But what if you get stuck?" asked Luz.

"Then go back to your profile, go back to your day-in-the-life. Re-read them. And then go back to your script and ask yourself "What would this character say if that character said 'I love you?' He might say 'I love you' too, but if you listen to him he might say 'Cut that sappy junk.' And you'll know it's right. You'll know because the character will have led you."

Apprehensive, excited, and determined, the kids began writing. Some, like Kim and Jasmine, started right away and didn't stop till the period ended. Clarence took his time, re-reading everything in his envelope and only writing a half page of dialogue. Venus, Monique, and Saul started quickly and bogged down. (One at a time, I told them to re-read the wishes in the profiles and the wish at the end of the day-in-the-life.) Felix started slowly but began to gain momentum as the period moved to its end.

❦

"Are you aware of your attitude towards Kim?" asked Ms. Finney.

"Sure. I think she's wonderful. She also may have real talent. She's the only one I'm going to urge to try writing professionally."

"You favor her," said Ms. Finney.

"I took your suggestion of seeing her alone—"

"I think the other children—"

"Maria Margarita and Monique are jealous."

"Well, maybe they have reason to be."

"No. I give them full attention. Maybe today I shouldn't have 'given' Maria Margarita the answer—I should have helped her discover it— but the real question here is what about a kid who has genuine talent? If a child did well in math, you would compliment her, wouldn't you? Why not compliment artistic impulses?"

"There are degrees."

"Just as there are degrees in 'constructive criticism.'"

"What does that mean?"

"I think you're on my case. Finding fault. Not listening to the overall development here. Only to the minor flaws. Last week I was so busy fending off your minor criticisms I couldn't even tell you why we start with writing about things we don't understand."

"What do you want? A pat on the back for everything that works? Or help with problem areas?"

"It's the tone, Ms. Finney, and you know it. What offends you so much?"

"Look, Mr. Sklar, you and I see things differently. Which is fine. But you have to remember: you are in my classroom. I work with these children all week. Every week. You come on Wednesdays. For twenty weeks. Some of the things you encourage complement things I do. Others don't."

"Like what?"

"Like discussing your domestic situation."

"I'm trying to set an example of openness."

"I understand that. But it doesn't mean there aren't consequences. Also, the time you take could be used for other things. . . ." Ms. Finney paused and we looked at each other. Finally, she continued. "But on balance I think what you do is good. For the children. So I want you here. Surely, you realize that."

"Yes."

"And as to my 'tone'—well, that's me. The kids live with it. My husband lives with it. My own kids live with it. Why can't you?"

"I was beginning to think it was personal."

"No, I really think your relationship with Kim is...important. But you should be aware of it. That girl is very lonely. The other kids, they...she's not popular. I worry about her," said Ms. Finney. She got up to get more coffee.

I looked at Ms. Finney. She was wearing her tweed suit, but her usual tough, business-like demeanor seemed to waver. I said, "I don't want to hurt her relationship with the other kids. But I really feel she has something special. Maybe I should bring her aside more. Cut down on the revelations in class."

"Yes, that's all I mean. I want her to have a chance too," said Ms. Finney and she turned away. Was she crying? I chose not to look.

Had I been overly sensitive? Had I ruined my relationship with Ms. Finney, even as I had been bragging about our wonderful teacher-training dynamic? More important, why did I feel compelled to reveal myself? I felt raw as I headed home.

I tried to think of similar incidents but found nothing but self-indulgence. Finally, I tried to treat my indiscretion as I would treat one from a kid: cut the blame and focus on what happened and why.

In effect, I had "acted out." My loneliness had popped out in the classroom. And why? Because Kim seemed to feel the same way? But why today? Was Ms. Finney's approval a factor? What about my inability to get my own work produced?

The answers obviously lay deep and might only be revealed by psychotherapy or the like. What could I do now? More important, could I ever avoid "acting out" completely? No. The question really was "How could I deal with those moments when I 'acted out'?" One clue came from the memory of an incident in a small town in Georgia.

I came to that town of 600 as an artist-in-residence. The Georgia Council for the Arts and the local community set me up nicely there, but my life became lonely. So when I was invited by my principal to go to her church and come home for Sunday dinner, I accepted with pleasure. The principal, a warm person and one of the most gifted administrators I have ever worked for, belonged to a "born-again" Christian church. As I was a guest, I planned to reserve judgement. The sermon, which focused on the man's role as initiator in the family, fascinated me. The general notion behind the sermon seemed perfectly valid. But when the minister began giving examples, he said, "Well, women drivers — what else can I say?" And "My wife, my own wife, painted a kitchen cabinet and then dissolved in tears when I didn't give the right reaction." He gave no stereotypical examples of men's behavior (they drink in bars, get into fights, beat their wives). It was only the women who were ridiculed under the guise of humor and education. The congregation loved it.

When we got to the principal's home, I wanted to discuss the sermon — to point out the way a perfectly valid idea was vitiated by sexist examples — but the phone rang and the principal was told her mother was sick. So we never discussed the sermon.

Back at school, I felt even more isolated and found myself determined to help the girls, especially the black girls in that mixed community. My first opportunity came when I chose kids for a "core" group that I would work with intensively. The core kids were usually the best actors and writers, but if a child might benefit particularly from being part of the special group, I could include him or her. So I chose a girl who did the exercises well but seemed shy and, from the look of her clothes, was quite poor. She, a girl who never was chosen for anything, became part of the elite core group. As we developed our play, she did well enough, but the day of the performance, she said she wouldn't be coming back to the school. She had no ride. I volunteered to take her and she agreed, but seemed anxious.

When I finally found her house, way back in the country on dirt roads some twenty miles from school, she wasn't there. Her mother said she was working "down the road." I found her collecting pecans in the dark. It turned out that we arrived in time for the show, where she performed beautifully.

Had I chosen this unlikely girl because of my frustration vis-à-vis the sermon? Had I almost created another uncomfortable — and possibly humiliating — experience for her? The answers were yes. But, as I thought about it afterwards, regardless of my motive and the frustrations I may have exposed the girl to, there were other issues. And just as I could make a psychological case against myself—my psycho-political motives—I could make a similar case for giving this girl a chance and against knee-jerk conservatism (these poor black kids shouldn't waste their time on artsy stuff; stick to the basics, prepare them for trades, etc.). What mattered was what we did. And what we did worked.

At home in Greenwich Village, I related this memory to the day's lesson: both situations stressed going moment to moment and trusting that something interesting would emerge. The lesson taught an approach to writing action that mirrored action as it happens in life. A certain amount of uncertainty and even danger is implicit. I had used myself as an example in class, just as I had taken the extra time with the girl in Georgia. In Georgia, I emerged heroic and in the Bronx a bit foolish, but both came from real impulses, and that encouraged the kids to take chances, to go beyond the easy and predictable. To listen to themselves. To get to the source of good writing.

This realization made me feel even better about the technique and the work with Kim and Maria Margarita and Monique. And Ms. Finney. I didn't know what would happen, but I would somehow coordinate my commitment to Kim with fairness to the other kids, just as I would re-establish my working relationship with Ms. Finney.

13.

ACTION

The kids wanted to dispense with the warm-up exercises so they would have more time for writing, but I asked, "Have you forgotten why we exercise? Why? Why do we do it?"

Nobody raised a hand, but fearing Kim might, I asked Felix. He, if anybody, should have remembered.

"I'm already relaxed," he said, not wanting to give me the satisfaction of a straight answer.

"But you could be even more relaxed. And what would be the point of that? Why relax?" I said, "Hector?" without waiting for a volunteer.

"I don't know."

"Who are we learning about when we write this play? Whose feelings are important here?"

"The characters," said Kim.

"Yes, but where do the characters come from?"

"Us? Our imagination," Kim said.

"Right. And that's why we exercise. So it's easier to get at and express our feelings. They get locked up in everyday life. We need to let them out each time. OK, is everybody set on that?"

The kids nodded, so I said, "We're also going to talk about action. Who can tell me about action? Monique?"

"Action? It's something happening."

"Right, and in a play we have a special way of making something happen. How many remember the 'broken light' improv?" I looked at a sea of raised hands. "In that one a boy wanted to run away, but the other said, 'Let's go to the principal.' Those are what we call 'wishes' in our profiles. But that's just a way of saying it's what they wanted most. Or what some actors call 'objectives.' Then what happened? Can you remember, Luz?"

"They fought," said Luz.

"Right, and fighting is what? Who can remember the word? Maria Margarita?"

"Conflict," she said with great pleasure.

"Yes, a form of conflict, just as that example about the boy and girl in the McDonald's is another form. Remember that one? He wants her to ask him out and she wants him to ask her. So they're in conflict, but they're not yelling and screaming at each other. And then what happened? In the improv. Hiram?"

"In mine, she gave in."

"Yes, and 'giving in' is action," I said. "It's a change in her feelings. And that's the way we write plays. Characters want something from each other. They come into conflict. And then there's action or change in feelings. That cycle is called a 'beat.' Which is a little like a chapter in a book. It's a complete section of a play," I said, and wrote the following on the board:

Beat

WANTING
CONFLICT
ACTION (CHANGE)

"But action isn't always a change in feelings," said Luis.

I hadn't heard from him in a while and I was quite curious. "How do you mean, Luis?"

"Well, if a car chases another car, what's that got to do with feelings?"

"Excellent question. And the answer is that the feelings change when the bad guy bashes into a wall or takes a wrong turn, just as they change when the good guy brakes for a pedestrian or catches up. But the important thing to remember here is that we are writing a play, not a movie. In a play we work more on the feelings that happen between people. Now let me give you one more example and then we'll warm up — were you afraid I'd forget to warm up? — and do some writing."

"Finally," said Maria Margarita.

"Think about a situation where you want to go outside and your mother or dad wants you to clean the bathroom. What are the wishes, what's the conflict, what's the action?"

"The wishes are 'to go outside' and 'to punish. . . .'" said Luz.

"Who said anything about 'punish'?" I asked. "Maybe the parents —"

"This is my play, my feelings," Luz snapped, and everybody laughed.

"All right. And the conflict?"

"Who's going to be the boss?" she said.

"Yes, excellent. And the action?"

"Dad gives in."

"Terrific. Now Clarence, would you lead the warm-up today? You can use any exercise. Show us something you do."

Clarence stood up and took the class through jumping jacks, push-ups, and sit-ups. And then we got down to work.

I circulated and found Deana not working. She didn't know how to start. I asked her what her characters wanted. She gave me a shrug and I said, "Well, you have it written down in two places. Look in your envelope and see what you find." "Oh, you mean on the day-in-the-life?" she said. "Yes," I answered, "and one other place." She thought a minute and said, "Profile." "Right," I answered. "Now check them out and I bet you'll know what to write." She got started.

I was happy to discover that both Luz and Yalmilka were working on the characters from their mother-daughter improv. Did they want to do their own plays or work together? I didn't usually allow that, I told them, but because they had seemed to work so well on the improv I would make an exception. Neither seemed ready to decide, so I told them to work on their own today and maybe they could collaborate later.

I circulated until just before the hour ended and asked all the kids to turn in their work. I wanted to see how they were doing in the beginning, to make sure they understood everything we had talked about.

Most of them seemed to get it, but there was a disturbing tendency for all the conflict to degenerate into name-calling and the action to be mired in insults. For example, in Elizabeth's play one character says, "You're stupid" and is answered with "You're ugly." To which the first character says, "Stupid's worse than ugly." And the next rejoinder is "No it's not." Which leads to "Yes it is." "No, it's not," etc.

Or the action came too quickly. For example, in Monique's play Grandma says, "You're going to visit your mother today," and the girl, who hates her mother, says, "OK." She doesn't whine or bargain or defy. She just gives in.

Also there seemed to be a confusion as to the next step after an action. So that's what I opened the next session with: how beats ascend and become scenes.

"Have you ever noticed how a good play or movie gets more and more exciting?" I asked at the beginning of the next class. The kids nodded and I said, "That's because the beats are ascending. Does anybody know what 'ascending' means?"

Nobody did. "It means leading up, the way a staircase leads up. It gets higher and higher," I said, indicating imaginary steps. "More and more important. And that's what our plays have to do. To ascend. Each beat leads to a higher or more important beat."

Blank faces stared back at me. I had to get more specific — fast. "Take that example about a child going out versus doing the chores." I said. "If the first acton is that the child says 'I hate you' and starts to run to his room, the second action has to top that. Maybe the mother not only refuses to let the child go, but also grounds him. Which makes the child take a more drastic action; he runs to his father. Which may lead to a conflict between mother and father, with the father storming out. You see how it builds?"

"It's like we're climbing up to the roof so we can see the whole city," said Kim. She hadn't raised her hand. The image just popped to the surface.

"But why?" asked Maria Margarita. "Why does every play have to be the same?"

"What do you mean?" I asked, genuinely curious.

"Why does every play have to be the same? Why do we have to do it the same way?"

"That's a good question. And there are many writers who have also asked it. They are always experimenting to find other ways, new ways. They are what's called the *avant-garde*, which is French for 'out ahead.' But before they find new ways, they learn the old ways. It's a little like building a house, Maria Margarita: you have to learn what makes most houses stand and then you can build a whole new way."

The house analogy seemed to work for Maria Margarita, so I went on to explain about scenes and acts. "A scene changes when a beat or a series of beats climaxes and the curtain goes down, or a character leaves or a new character enters. An act is a series of scenes that builds to a new climax and ends in the curtain being drawn."

The kids found the technical concepts of scenes and acts difficult to grasp, so I decided to let it go. They would discover it naturally. If they wrote beats and made them ascend, the scenes and acts would follow.

After reading some of the works-in-progress, I decided to work on the issues of insults and quick action. "Luz and Felix, would you come up in front?" I whispered in Felix's ear that Luz had snitched on him to the teacher and he should make her admit it. And in Luz's ear, I whispered that she wanted to dismiss him from her presence; he was like a bug to her. She would never do anything for or against him.

They started their improv and soon it degenerated into "did too" versus "did not." Finally, I stopped them and said, "Now here we have two of our best actors, but what happened when they kept arguing? What did you feel?"

"Bored," said Hiram.

"Why?"

"Well, they kept saying the same thing."

"Exactly," I said. "Remember: action is a change of emotion, not a repetition. If you keep repeating your conflict without allowing it to *ascend*, it will be boring."

With that thought clearly introduced, I set up another improv between Felix and Luz. This time I had her say, "Come home, Momma's waiting" and he says, "OK!"

They did it and the audience waited. Finally Luz turned and said, "That's it." And I pointed out how that was too little conflict. How he could have said "Wait a minute." Or "You're a momma's girl." And she could have attacked him.

"Now, before you start on any new beat, go back over your old ones and see if they are too short or too long. And when you're satisfied, go on. Write as many beats as you want. Just make sure they ascend."

Ms. Finney and I were cautious with each other, and when she mentioned how Clarence had a nice authority when he led the exercises, I agreed. I would now have each child take a turn, I said. It would help to build a sense of responsibility. Also, I was running out of exercises, I admitted, smiling.

"But it might not be as relaxing as the stretches. All those push-ups," she said, smiling back.

The joke about push-ups seemed to take the edge off. I said, "Hmmm.

Maybe I can do a breathing stretch first. And then turn it over to the exercise leader."

"Yes. Now what was that with Yalmilka and Luz?"

"I thought they might like to collaborate, but they didn't seem very excited about it."

"Wanted to make their own choices?"

"Yes. Hopefully. But collaboration can work. I did it with a couple of fourth-grade classes. In those cases it was tactical. There were thirty-four kids in one and thirty-three in the other and it was only a ten-week course. If we would have tried to produce even five plays it would have been total chaos. When they collaborated, each was responsible for a character and they took turns, as they would in conversation. And, in the end, we had eighteen short plays that they could read in front of the class."

"So they didn't memorize lines and wear costumes?"

"No. There wasn't time or space."

"Yes, we know that story here," said Ms. Finney.

After a pause, I said, "What is it with Maria Margarita? Where does that sense of betrayal come from?"

"I think it's one of those classic father things. Well, not so classic. Her father didn't exactly abandon them. He apparently went back to Puerto Rico. He couldn't stand it here. He wanted them to come with him, but her mother, who was born here, tried living there once and now won't do it again."

"How do you know all this stuff?" I asked.

"The kids talk to me. So do some parents. And the other teachers talk to younger brothers and sisters."

"I'm going to try to see her alone too."

"That would be good," said Ms. Finney.

I caught up with Maria Margarita in the schoolyard during lunch and brought her to Ms. Finney's empty classroom, where the clear, early spring sunlight was shining through the window.

"Do you know why I wanted to see you?" I asked.

"No," she said. She seemed more afraid than hostile.

"You seem worried about your play. Are you?"

"No." She looked down at her sneakers. They were blue running shoes without a name-brand label.

"I also wanted you to know how much I like it. Even more than the rest of your work. Which, as you know, is excellent."

Maria Margarita stole a glance.

"What's special about your play is your passion. Your characters feel so much. They care. And we care about them."

"It's really about my father."

"Well, he seems like a very loving man."

"But he's so unfair."

"People can be wrong and also love. And they can learn."

"He can't."

"But in the play, it's a character, not your father. The character can do anything."

"He can't learn, either—the character. That's the way he is, too."

"All right. Just as long as you know the difference between the character and your father."

"I do," she snapped.

"And there's something else: if you can help us understand why he can't learn, you will be doing us all—including yourself—a great service."

"But I don't know."

"Keep writing. Let the characters lead you. You'll find it."

She looked again.

"I believe in your work. I believe in you. Now go to lunch," I said, knowing I had finally hit the right chord with her.

After she left, I went over to the window. Patches of green had appeared on the empty lots between the school and the housing project three blocks away.

14.

DIALOGUE

The next three sessions the kids tried to listen to their characters and to transform desires, conflicts, and actions into dialogue.

They also began to enjoy each other's warm-ups. After Clarence's successful, if strenuous, session, I asked Elizabeth to show us some dance stretches from her ballet class. After Elizabeth there were volunteers galore. Leading exercises — especially new ones from sports, paramilitary groups, TV work-outs, and Mom's specialties — created genuine interest.

After the warm-ups, the sessions became intense. Some of the kids wrote easily and well. Others struggled. Still others had good and bad days. And a couple were threatened by the process. Ms. Finney and I circulated and helped each child, but some had to wait longer than they would have liked.

Ironically, one of the children having a difficult time was Luz. Clearly the best actor — as well as being a beautiful, mature child — she resisted writing. At first, I asked her what the characters wanted and she gave me quick, clear answers, so I said, "Think of that each time a character is ready to speak." "I just can't," she said, so I reminded her how the words seemed to flow from her mouth when she and Yalmilka improvised. "This is different," she said. But when I pressed her to find out why, she could only say she was an actor, that she was content to let others write. When I suggested that the story she had to tell was special, she grew impatient. To her it was "stupid." Who cared about a "mean" woman and a "spoiled brat."

As Luz talked more about the lead characters, it became clear that she found the material disturbing. She dismissed her characters as selfish, but her intensity made me feel she cared deeply. Finally I said, "I'm interested in those people. I want to know what they say to each other. Just go line by line. Beat by beat."

"But it'll be boring," said Luz. "They're such selfish, dumb — they would never understand each other. . . ."

"Well, what would make them change?" I asked.

"Nothing in this world," she said.

"Well, what about the next?" I said.

"I can't put heaven on the stage."

"Oh, yes you can. Or you could have a character come down from heaven. There's a famous play called *Our Town* where that happens." The notion of somebody coming down from heaven interested Luz, and soon she was writing furiously.

Jaime had a different problem. He believed in the character based on his brother, and felt good enough about the character who was based on a local hood. His problem was skills. Handwriting, spelling, grammar, the play format—each presented a daunting obstacle. He was nearly in tears when we finally talked.

Realizing I could not teach a private remedial course at that moment, I suggested that he write the story "his own way." We could "clean it up and put it in the proper format" later. His story came first, I assured him. "Just put it down any way you want." Wouldn't that put him "behind" the other kids, he wanted to know. "For a while, yes, but once you know what's going to happen you can copy it over in the right format quickly. I'll see that you get an extra period to do the copying." Reassured, he began to work.

Maria Margarita worked fast, but she ran into a common problem for beginning playwrights: her characters spoke as they do in real life. Dialogue is different from conversation. In conversation, character A might ask character B how he felt, and character B would answer and inquire about character A's health. Even though character B seethed with anger. In dramatic dialogue we go directly to the feelings we hide. So I suggested that Maria Margarita let the characters bypass the polite chitchat and go directly to their wishes or desires. "Dialogue is not what people would actually say," I told her, "but what they want to say in their secret heart. So, when character A says, 'How are you?' character B might say, 'That blouse is yukkie.' To which character A might say, 'You are the rudest person I know. . . .'"

This point seemed so important that I stopped the class and had Jasmine and Monique do the character A and character B scene. Immediately it became clear how going directly to expressing wishes condensed the action. "That," I explained, "is why a play that takes two hours can tell about a whole family crisis that brews for six months—or sixteen years. As playwrights we go right to the deepest feelings. We don't waste time."

When I finally came to Kim, she was ready to deal with "why." "Why does this character want to leave home?" I asked her. "Because of him. Her father," said Kim, a little impatient. "Yes, but what does he do that makes her so mad?" Kim started to answer, but I stopped her and said, "Put all that in a scene. If we see him doing that to her on stage—instead of her complaining about it to her mother—we know why. If this is the important action of the play—her going away—we have to see it happening in front of us. That's the beauty of a play: it allows us to feel what the characters feel. But only if we see the action on stage. That's the difference between knowing why and really understanding why."

"But where does that scene go?"

"Ah, now you're ready to do a step chart," I said. "A step chart is like an outline. You take a fresh sheet of paper and you list every beat, how long it is, and what happens in it. So, for example, let's take your first three beats:

1. Mom and Denise talk about chores and Dad.
   a. Length: 3 pages.
   b. Action: Denise runs to her room.
2. Denise talks to Damarus, the bird.
   a. Length: ½ page.
   b. Action: Denise decides to run away.
3. Mom and Dad fight.
   a. Length: ¾ page.
   b. Action: Mom gives in (Denise overhears).
4. Mom and Denise fight about Dad.
   a. Length: 2 pages.
   b. Action: Mom sees how bad Dad is, and Denise runs away.

"When you look at this chart, it's easier to see where your new big scene goes—and you can decide what other rewriting you might want to do."

"What do you mean?" asked Kim.

"Well, look at how many pages the scene between Mom and Dad is. Less than one. Maybe there's more between them, more Denise should hear. And that might help decide where the big new scene should go.

"Another way to tell where it goes is to trace how the actions happen. If you just look at the actions, you see the main points and it's easier to decide where to put the new scene."

Kim was writing her new step chart by the time I had risen from my squat beside her desk.

Yalmilka had finished her play when I arrived. It wasn't as strong as Kim's or Maria Margarita's or Luz's, which dealt with the same subject matter, because Yalmilka had a tendency to make her beats short, indicating wanting and conflict in one or two lines instead of realizing them fully in five or six. But the actions ascended to a climax that made the characters change. She had done it and I wanted to congratulate her and validate her work before I asked for rewrites. "OK, now what's the title?" Yalmilka hadn't thought about it. So I suggested that she do just that. "A title," I explained when she gave me a blank stare, "says what the whole thing is about. If a story is about a girl and a boy, the title might use their names, like Shakespeare does with *Romeo and Juliet*."

I had to explain who Romeo and Juliet were to Yalmilka, so I brought the whole class in on the explanation of Shakespeare and his play—and the problem of titles.

"Now if the play were about them getting married, it might be called *The Marriage of Romeo and Juliet*, but it's not about marriage, it's about their whole lives, including their deaths, so it's about all of them. Just as the TV show 'Family Ties' is about just that, what keeps a family together. The same thing is true about books. Let's take an example. Who has a favorite book?"

Jasmine said, *"The Chronicles of Narnia,"* and I said, "Great. Those are tales about that special world. The title tells us everything. If you're uncomfortable about a friendship, maybe friendship could be in the title. If it's about a new friendship, then 'new' might be in the title. Think about what your play means."

When I came back to Yalmilka, she said her title was *Growing Up*. That seemed like a fine title to me.

Clarence, who worked in the same abbreviated way Yalmilka did, finished and found a title quickly too. His was *The Big Game*. I liked that as well and said, "Now you two are ready for rewrites."

I asked them to make step charts and then look at their plays, beat by beat, and tell me how each beat could be fuller. "For example, in your play, Clarence, when the coach says, 'Stay late for practice,' the boy hesitates and then says, 'OK.' But maybe he could explain to the coach that he has to babysit for his little sister. And then the coach might say

'That's your problem.' And the boy could say 'Don't you care about me?' And the coach could say. . . . Do you see how it can develop? Let it grow bigger, reveal more things. And therefore the audience understands more, cares more. And, Yalmilka, think about the scene where the mother says she can't afford to buy the shoes; now the girl says OK, but maybe she could say 'You have money for your own clothes. Or my little sister's clothes.' And then the mother could explain how clothes are important for her job or something. Do you see?"

She and Clarence nodded and started rewriting.

During the period, Ms. Finney had gone from child to child as I had. When I first asked her to do this she had said no, asserting that she couldn't help the kids with the "creative business." But when I assured her again that all the creativity comes from the kids, that all she had to do was ask questions—what did the characters want, what were they afraid of, etc.—and maybe correct the play format, she agreed. And, of course, she was wonderful because she listened to what the kids said and she responded naturally. But after the third day of circulating, she said, "There should be ten of us."

That reminded me of the 52nd Street Project, a group I had been working with after school. The Project, begun in 1982 by Willie Reale, dedicates itself to reversing the ratio of kids to adults. Willie believes that children in general and the kids of Clinton (formerly Hell's Kitchen, on Manhattan's West Side) in particular crave adult contact. And when they get it, as they do in the Project's various programs, they feel better about themselves. They also get the validation of an adult audience for their work in the theater because the project attracts adults from all over the city.

Ms. Finney wanted to know where the adults came from, so I explained how Willie, as a writer-director-actor, had brought his friends from the theater world to the Project and they volunteered in between theater or film jobs.

Ms. Finney was quite intrigued by all this, but soon we were back to the reality of P.S. 34. The 52nd Street Project works with a limited number of kids and an almost unlimited number of adults. There were thirty-two kids in Ms. Finney's class and two of us. We could only do what we could do.

Ms. Finney then mentioned the exercises Saul had introduced. They came from a paramilitary group he belonged to. The discipline it offered seemed to touch Saul in a way similar to the way the Project touched the kids on 52nd Street, she said.

I had to agree. And for that matter, I said, so did gangs. And drugs. And they were with the kids many more hours than we. That thought made me sad.

And then Ms. Finney, the tough realist, spoke. "But you know, if Luz continues to deal with the mother-daughter feelings as she has so far, that's—well I think she's really growing."

Thinking about our sober conversation in La Taza de Azul, I stiffened my resolve to make this playwriting course as significant as I could. And that meant doing the serious production Mr. Hyman and I had talked about.

So why was I so uneasy? Possibly because of the memory of a production I did with junior high kids in Brooklyn. That production had been part of a mixed-media program. A dancer, a sculptor, and I had agreed to teach our respective arts and then create a performance that integrated all three.

The production had been a great success, but I had felt dissatisfied with my role. The plays the kids wrote had been slight and their interest in doing the show had been lackluster. I had pushed and pulled them along to this great show and they were pleased at the end. But they had learned very little. It would have been better, I felt, to spend more time on process and less on product.

Examining my work with that group, I realized how difficult a situation it had been. Each of us was working with around sixty kids. The teachers, overwhelmed by their own obligations, hardly took part. The kids themselves, an odd mix of middle-class drop-outs from private schools and poor kids bussed to a wealthy neighborhood, were hostile to each other and to the teachers. My response—to make the show happen regardless—had been about my determination, not about the kids. Afterwards I felt resentful about Big Shows and Results.

But that was an easy position for me to take, I had to admit, as I finished my *cafe con leche*. Too many people in the United States err in the direction of product and "bottom line." I go in the other direction, almost making a fetish of process. But in fact, most of my own experience with productions had been excellent. What about the 52nd Street Project? What about the show in Macon? What about countless other productions? And more important, what about these kids? Their work deserved a production. The process in this case demanded a production.

On that note, I headed for the door, waving to an amused Carmen. I assumed I had been "intense" again. Well, spring makes us all a bit odd. That would be my excuse.

HEARING IT

As each child finished his play, chose a title, and did a rewrite, I said, "Think about who you want to play the parts." Ms. Finney had also arranged a deal with the computer teacher: as children finished writing, they began typing the plays onto disks from which they would make clean copies for the actors.

So in the next couple of sessions some kids wrote, some did step charts, some chose titles, some did rewrites, some typed, some began casting and rehearsing their plays.

These sessions became a bit chaotic, but we always warmed up together at the beginning and did readings at the end. Also, Ms. Finney and I circulated and helped kids who were frustrated or needed some other kind of special attention. By the third session — due to some extra computer time arranged yet again by Ms. Finney — we were doing readings full-time.

Before the readings began, I announced that every play would be read, but only five would be given full productions, and that Ms. Finney and I would choose the five.

Felix said that wasn't fair. Others agreed.

I explained that I only had twenty sessions to work with them — there simply wasn't time to do thirty-two plays, but if they wanted to carry on by themselves maybe they could do the rest later in the year.

Ms. Finney, speaking from her desk at the back of the room, said that would be difficult; the class has many other subjects to cover.

I pointed out that those who did not have their plays done would be actors or directors or stagehands; everybody would have a job in the production. We would not be choosing the five "best" plays but rather the ones that best composed an evening, e.g., all plays about family, or all comedies, or two comedies, one mystery, and two dramas.

Saul asked if he could work the spotlight. I said that was a possibility. Ms. Finney and I would have to work out the jobs, once we knew whose plays were being done. Everybody could state preferences.

Other kids asked about acting and stagehand work and even directing (when I explained the director is the boss on the set), but there were
still kids who felt doing only five plays was unfair. Felix and Maria Margarita in particular.

We were at an impasse, so I asked for suggestions. How would they
handle it, given the limited time? After much discussion, the kids voted
for Ms. Finney and me to select the five best plays, but only after we
had heard them all read. That would give each play its best shot.

We did the reading simply: the actors sat on chairs in front of the
class. An extra actor read the stage directions. The playwright sat in the
audience. (I wanted the playwright to hear his or her play without worrying about having to act too.) I encouraged the actors to listen to each
other and to respond as simply as possible. We wanted to hear the
playwright's words. When each play was done, I asked the other kids
to describe the main event.

For example, when we read Luz's play, Maria Margarita and Yalmilka
played mother and daughter and Venus played Grandma, the character
from heaven. The three actors sat next to each other and Luz stayed
in her seat. Luz had wanted to play the Mom, but I assured her that
listening to the words would help her see how wonderful her work was—
in addition to allowing her to hear the wrong notes. Venus, Maria Margarita, and Yalmilka read well, and the kids quickly understood Luz's
crucial point: that the mother had not wanted the child at the time of
conception.

As might be expected, the kids who had acted well in the improvs
gave strong performances—except those who read poorly. Felix, a fine
actor in an improv, read badly (later with the lines memorized he would
be a superlative actor). He simply could not follow the words in Kim's
crucial father-daughter scene. (That, of course, upset Kim, and we spent
the good part of a private session talking about the inevitable differences
between actors and writers.) Others, like Benny and Victor, refused to
do readings. Ms. Finney and I agreed to let them refuse. There would
be plenty of backstage jobs. If Benny and Victor wrote and then worked
as stagehands, that would be a real success.

The range and scope—not to mention the quality of the writing—
thrilled me. Maria Margarita's friendship play had evolved into a divorce

play (that's why the friend had been behaving so oddly). Jaime's play, with special help from Ms. Finney, had been transformed into a mystery drama: the neighborhood punk, a flunky for a group of gangsters, leads the brother character to a cache of money hidden in a basement and the two really face each other. Luis' characters were computers (a nice development from his object character) in a wonderful comedy about the confusions created by talking computers. Luz made the mother-daughter-dead grandmother conflict into a García Lorca-style tragedy, while Yalmilka made hers into a snappy TV sketch.

The children had let the characters speak, and real plays had emerged.

Ms. Finney felt we should do all the plays. She asked if there wasn't something else we could do. Something in between a full production and the reading.

I explained that we could do staged readings. The actors could learn "blocking" (stage movements) and act as much as they could with the scripts in their hands. But that would take rehearsal too.

"Maybe," I thought aloud, "the other plays — or some of them — could be done as part of an after-school program."

"No," said Ms. Finney, "the school closes up tight at four. Nobody's allowed to stay. What we need is a way to do the plays without much rehearsal but have it be more special, more satisfying than a reading."

"Are there any free periods? I mean we're already into computer time. Maybe we could get the art or music teachers involved."

"We don't have any. Welcome to budget cutbacks."

At that point I felt we needed a *deus ex machina*, but none arrived. We simply agreed to think about the problem and Ms. Finney rushed back to class.

Passing the school's pay phone, I remembered I had to call Teachers & Writers about my hours. Elizabeth Fox, T&W's Program Director, answered, and when she asked how it was going, I explained what Ms. Finney wanted and how I didn't think it was possible. Elizabeth said "videotape" before I could finish whining. "Don't you remember the artists' meeting when we talked about all those options for culminating events?" she asked with a devilish tone that seemed to crackle through the telephone wire.

I caught up with Ms. Finney at three. She loved the idea, especially when I said we could tape readings. We wouldn't need rehearsal for that. We sat down at her desk to plan.

Ms. Finney thought she could wangle a video camera from the district office. She also said it would be a wonderful way to reach the students who might miss the plays. That got me thinking about an experiment that was part of the Henry Street Settlement's artist-in-residence program.

In one class at a Henry Street school, they taped plays on audiocassettes and broadcast them through the school on the P.A. system, late on Friday afternoons.

Quite excitedly, Ms. Finney and I worked out a system: we would do five plays as a full production, five as staged readings (for kids who would come early), ten plays on videotape as readings, and the balance as radio plays. We also agreed to meet over the weekend to choose plays and assign other jobs. By 4 P.M., when I walked Ms. Finney to her green Volvo station wagon, we had a plan.

As I sat in my apartment watching a late March snowstorm, the challenge of our schedule reminded me of the organizing effort I had made in Macon, when people from all over the community had mobilized and worked together. But soon I realized significant differences. In Macon, key adults had been wanting to start a theater for years. Here we would have to generate the enthusiasm. Also, the people we would call upon would be involved in many other projects. Ms. Finney's contact at the district office might get us a video camera, but who would do the taping? And what about the sets? I might ask an artist friend to design them, but she could not supervise their construction. Who, in fact, would help build the sets and props? And music? Who would arrange for incidental music? And what about money? We could get some things donated, but there are hidden expenses in a production, and the community here in the Bronx was not rich or well organized.

As my questions swirled, I realized we could be heading towards a fiasco. That was unacceptable. The kids had come too far. I had to find a way to make it all happen — successfully.

What I had to do was make an inventory of resources and possibilities. And then do the best we could. Accept the limitations — and make them work to our advantage. For example, if adults were unavailable to build the sets, we would limit the design, have kids do it all and bill the sets as "Made by Students."

The primary lesson in off-off-Broadway theater productions — priorities — suddenly seemed invaluable. A play can be enhanced by sets, lights, and costumes. It also can become *about* sets, lights, and costumes. A play can be enhanced by acting and directing, or become *about* acting and directing. It's the producer's job to decide what's the best way to enhance the play, given physical resources, time, and support staff.

To that end, I started with myself. How much time could I donate and still maintain my income and sanity? What about my commitment to other schools? To my work as a writer? My social life? I could short-change all those things somewhat, but not for eight straight weeks. I needed a specific structure. I could, for example, work early on three mornings because I taught at two other schools nearby and could take cabs. I also could stay after school on Wednesdays to help recruit parents. But anything more would produce diminishing returns; I would get resentful and therefore less effective.

I had to get a time commitment from Ms. Finney, and to see what support the principal and local board could offer. Teachers & Writers would help; maybe they could hire a video artist. There also was the Bronx Council on the Arts — maybe it could do something. Perhaps there was a way to eke out more rehearsal time in another space. A local church perhaps. Or borrow resources such as spotlights. In that way, this production could be like the one in Macon. I would ask everybody to make suggestions as well as to contribute specific items. I would ask them to join us.

But mostly I needed a commitment from the kids. They had to understand what a serious project we were embarking upon. They had to understand that the production was theirs, but at the same time they would need to share it with others. Could I do that in a speech or series of speeches? No, that would not be enough. The kids needed to take an active role. They had to understand what was necessary, and what they had to do. I would ask them to sign a contract the way I had the kids from the 52nd Street Project sign a contract.

The 52nd Street contract was divided into privileges and obligations. On the one hand the kids were guaranteed productions of their plays; on the other, they were obliged to do rewrites and take part in rehearsals. If they failed in their obligations they would lose their privileges. The 52nd Street kids, who knew the privileges, agreed on and fulfilled their obligations.

In another case, at a junior high in Brooklyn, the contract included the right of the kids to charge money and divvy up the box office afterwards. That incentive created interest, but afterwards I felt uncomfortable about it. With many of the kids the money became an end in itself.

In the production of the video of *The Twins in the Lobby*, all the principal actors got copies of the tape.

Now I asked the P.S. 34 kids to agree to come to rehearsals prepared and to work diligently during the designated time. In exchange they would get five plays in full productions, the staged readings, the videos, and the radio plays. And at the end, we would go on a special trip to a Broadway theater.

I still wished that I could induce the kids to come without a specific "reward," that they would work for the pleasure of the work itself. But, as Ms. Finney and I agreed, that might come later. First they had to experience the pleasure of working. The incentives I offered would help them stick with the production until they saw the work itself as the real reward.

16.

PROTOCOL

By the following Monday night Ms. Finney and I had chosen the five plays. The kids had charged us to pick the best plays instead of creating a balanced evening, so the task, difficult in any event, led to some real soul searching. How important was mastery of technical problems, like creating a series of ascending beats? What about character development and dialogue? And the value of an honestly probed feeling, like betrayal? Or an ambitious, dangerous topic, like a dying parent? We struggled with these issues for a week and finally weighted a deeply probed feeling higher than a courageous choice and a courageous choice a shade higher than technical success. We felt character development and dialogue ranked about equally with the structure of beats.

After class that Tuesday, Ms. Finney posted the choices and listed the assignments for acting roles, directors, and technical directors (the students who would be responsible for sets, costumes, and props).

When I arrived in class for our session at 10:20 on Wednesday, Monique raised her hand. She wanted to know why Luz would be acting in her own play. No other writer would be.

She was right and I had to say so. But I also said I had urged Luz to write this play, when all along she had said she wanted only to act. Now, after the class had charged us with choosing the best plays, I had no other choice but to pick hers. But I also felt obliged to cast her because from the first she said she wanted to act.

Monique absorbed this information impassively, as did the others.

I skipped on to auditions. We had bypassed auditions because of time considerations. Auditions, I explained, often work pretty much the way schoolyard games work. Captains—in this case the directors—choose friends or the "best players," but many kids aren't chosen or bat last and play right field.

"Luz gets to be captain, choose first, and bat first—but nobody else does," noted Monique with tight lips.

Feeling more and more mired, I said, "It seemed fair to me, but if you want to talk about it more after class, Monique, we will."

Monique did not respond, so I explained the role of the director. "The director," I said, "will be boss on the set. I will give copies of the plays to the directors. They will distribute them to the actors and make sure everybody has a comfortable place to sit and can see one another (I recommend that you put two tables together and put the chairs around), and will arbitrate all disputes about interpretation and judge complaints about other actors; no actor will be allowed to criticize another actor directly," I emphasized. If he or she didn't like another actor's choice for playing a particular line or scene, he or she could come to the director *after* a rehearsal.

"That's stupid," said Felix.

"Well, can anybody figure out why I am asking you to do such a 'stupid' thing?" When nobody volunteered, I said, "Think about games you play on the schoolyard. What if there were no boss, no captain, no teacher—what happens?"

"War!" shouted Jaime.

"Right," I said, "and we can't have war, if there are two hundred people sitting out there in the audience."

"Do you think we'll have two hundred people?" asked Hector.

"Maybe. But however many there are, we have to work together. And for that, somebody has to take charge."

"But what if you hate the director?" asked Hiram.

"Good question. I'm going to ask you to give the director a chance to be fair. And, directors, I expect you to be fair. But if the rest of you feel your director acts unfairly—if he or she is not listening to your complaints—then you can come to me or Ms. Finney. And we will talk to the director."

At first this seemed to satisfy everyone. Then Kim raised her hand: "What if you're the writer and the director doesn't do your play right?"

"Yes, that would be a problem. And it does happen. But I'm going to ask you to follow the same procedure, you writers. Let the director be in charge during the rehearsal. You can complain to him afterwards. And if you don't feel the director is listening to you, Ms. Finney and I are here. Also," I said a bit ironically, "next time *you* may be the director of *his* play when we do it for radio."

At that point I felt I had to make a speech. I said, "This protocol—this way of doing things—is strict, maybe stricter than on the teams you play on, because we're dealing with our truest, deepest emotions. You writers did it. And now the director, actors, and technical directors will do it. And when people deal with their truest, deepest feelings they get angry faster, they get upset faster, they get scared faster. We need protocol because there is so much feeling. Protocol allows us to express our feelings and know there will be order. It's a good word. Remember it: *protocol*," I said, and wrote it on the board.

Next, I designated five rehearsal areas around the room and one space for technical directors to meet; I indicated which group would use which area.

After that, I explained that the actors in each of the five groups would read their play once. They would then ask questions, if something wasn't clear. The director would answer, but if the director wanted to, he could ask the author to answer in his stead. Then when everybody understood the play, the actors would read it again.

Just before we broke up into groups, I asked the actors to "just read the words." Later, I explained, I would teach them more about acting. "But first, *listen to the words*, understand the words," I said. "Those words become the foundation for all your creative choices. Make your foundation strong."

I also asked the technical directors to sit and listen. Later, they would make their own creative decisions about the set, lights, props, make-up, and costumes. Today they, like the actors, would learn what the plays were about.

"But what if you're just doing lights?" said Saul.

"You're not *just* doing lights. You must make decisions about every technical part of your show. And every decision should make that play clearer. Including the lights. If, for example, you want to make the play look scary or spooky, you might use blue or green gels—the colored plastic sheets put over the lights to change the color—but if you wanted to make the play look cute and fun you might use pinks and oranges."

"We're going to get to do all that?" said Saul. He seemed excited.

"Only when you have a plan—in writing—that explains why you're choosing one color or another. And when that plan is okayed by your director."

At that point, we broke up into groups and the actors read the plays. Ms. Finney and I floated from one group to another, reinforcing the director's authority and urging the actors to deliver their lines straight.

The five plays were: 1) Kim's play about the father who comes and goes; 2) Luis' play about the computers; 3) Jaime's mystery play about the gangster gold; 4) Maria Margarita's play about the influence of divorce on a friendship; 5) Luz's mother-daughter-dead grandmother play.

The readings went well enough. Some of the kids had done the original readings and knew the plays already (Ms. Finney and I had tried to cast the author's choice whenever possible), others wanted to make a good impression. And the directors and technical directors seemed on best behavior. We made a tentative but solid first step.

Later that day at a lunch meeting I talked with the five authors. I wanted to reinforce the importance of their being chosen, to get their impressions of the readings, and to explain the equally important job they now had as playwrights watching their plays.

After I congratulated them, they gave me their impressions, which ranged from outrage to quiet satisfaction. I counseled patience. And respect. They had written the play, now other people would use the play as a springboard for other talents.

Kim did not like the springboard metaphor. Her play existed unto itself, she felt. The actors had to do it right. The other writers agreed. So I withdrew that image and said, "Respect their right to explore and to find the right way to do the play. It's a little like a teacher standing over you when you're figuring out a problem. Too much interference from the author makes the director, actors, and technical director nervous. And they won't do as well."

"But what are we supposed to do while they're 'figuring out the problem'?" Jaime wanted to know.

"There will be lots. For one, you can do rewrites if a section sounds wrong. For another, you can substitute for any of the actors or the director if someone gets sick. You can work with your technical director. You will be meeting with me individually to talk about what's happening."

"Can I build the computers?" asked Luis.

"If your technical director says OK. And, of course, you have to follow the technical director's plan. And that has to be OK'd by the director."

"The director really is the boss?" said Luz.

"Right. And why? Why do we need a 'boss'?" I asked. "What's the word?"

"Protocol," the five writers answered.

"That was a tough decision we made about Luz," said Ms. Finney. "Monique was not pleased."

"Probably none of them were. But Luz's play really is outstanding. That's what they asked us to choose."

"The question is her acting. Is it really that much better? Should we—"

"Yes," I answered. "There have been three really talented actors I've worked with over the last six years, during which I've worked with five hundred kids or more. The other two live in Georgia."

"But talent is such a vague notion."

"And yet we always know it," I said.

"Yes," said Ms. Finney, who proceeded to describe the moment she saw Dustin Hoffman in an off-Broadway show, shortly before he went on to make *The Graduate*. "I just wanted to watch him, I didn't know who he was or why I wanted to watch him—he wasn't that handsome— but I did."

"There are so very few people who have *it*."

"And you really think Luz does?"

"Yes, and she needs every break to develop it. Even if she had come from a home with all the advantages."

"Which she doesn't," said Ms. Finney.

"As I told you, I don't push kids into show business, but for Luz, it might make sense. I think we have a special responsibility to talented kids."

"Agreed. But what are we going to do about Monique?"

"I guess I have to talk to her."

"Pull her out of class next period."

Monique looked shy when we sat down in the teachers' lounge, so I decided to come straight to the point: "Do you still feel it's unfair to have Luz act, if she's having a play done?"

"Yes," snapped Monique.

I took a moment to look at her. She wore a grey skirt, white blouse, and black patent leather shoes. This was the first time she hadn't worn jeans since the second week.

"What would you do — given that you felt her play was the best?"

"Let somebody else act in it," said Monique.

"But she's a truly talented actress."

"If you do it for Luz, you should do it for Maria Margarita," pronounced Monique.

"So you feel it's favoritism. That's what you felt about Kim, too. Isn't it?"

I sensed Monique would not admit to this, so I changed tactics. "What about taking the matter to the class and voting? Ask them if I should choose another play, so Luz can act."

Monique looked at the ground. I continued, "Because I don't want to be unfair. And I don't want to short-change anybody who really tries and gives extra."

"I try. I give extra," said Monique, and suddenly she was crying.

"Yes," I said, surprised, as I put my arm around her, "and that's why I made you a director. That's why I put you with Maria Margarita: because you have the talent and the strength to do justice to her play. Ms. Finney thought it would be fun for you two to work together. When we do your play on the radio, Maria Margarita will direct it."

After a quiet moment, Monique, who remained nestled under my arm, asked, "How long did it take you to decide who did what?"

"Well, we met twice for a couple of hours. And of course we read the plays over and over on our own." This obviously was the right answer. Monique got up and blew her nose. Later, when we took the vote in class, she voted to let Luz both act and have her play done.

Later I wondered if I had done the right thing. At the time I was certain Monique wanted to be acknowledged, to feel that she too was special. She wanted fairness, but on a deeper level she wanted me to see who she really was. And when I told her Ms. Finney and I had taken so much time thinking about them, that need seemed satisfied.

But what about the issue of fairness? Couldn't I have found a way to choose Luz's play and have her act in a radio play or a staged reading, or arranged for private acting lessons the next year? And reached Monique another way? Now, I think I could have. My interest in nurturing Luz's talent may have been overzealous.

17.

BEING THE BOSS

"You're the bosses," I said to the five directors when we met before
school the following week. Cliff Vine, a college student from the New
School for Social Research, joined us at this meeting; he had been enlisted
as my assistant by Teachers & Writers. "But, as I said last week, you have
to listen to everybody and be fair. Otherwise the play will be lousy, and
that makes you a lousy boss."

The directors—Monique, Hector, Jasmine, Clarence, and Kim, who
was sitting in for Alberto, a quiet boy who was absent—digested this,
and I continued: "But a director does more than listen and be fair. You
have to take charge. You have to keep order and make sure everybody
works."

"But kids fool around," said Hector.

"Of course, that's why you're the boss."

"But they don't listen," said Jasmine. "What do you do then?"

"Who has any ideas?" I said.

"Punish 'em," said Clarence, and I thought about the extra laps the
coach in his play was always meting out.

"Or just bop 'em," said Hector. He seemed serious.

"What if they bop us back?" said Jasmine.

"Or they get mad and won't do anything?" said Kim.

At that point, I asked them how they themselves got "motivated." It
took a few moments to clarify the word and get the kids thinking (it
was 8 A.M.), but soon we began talking about self-interest and finally
Kim said, "We just have to tell them that they're the ones who are going
to look stupid if they're up in front of 200 people and they don't know
their lines." Interestingly enough, it was Monique who accentuated the
positive. She said, "You have to tell them how they're gonna love all that
applause."

Cliff, who wore a Bob Marley and the Wailers tee shirt, added that
as a kid he had been lazy about acting, and as a result he had forgotten
lines on the stage. It had been a horribly embarrassing experience and
he would be willing to tell any of the actors how important rehearsal

is. The directors listened to him with genuine interest.

The kids also appeared satisfied that they had developed a modus operandi, so I said, "What happens if they don't respond?" The directors seemed at a loss, so I suggested that they ask "why."

"Like you do," said Kim with a giggle.

"All the time," added Jasmine, also giggling.

"They know me too well," I said, smiling at Cliff. "Anyway, maybe your actor really is sick. Or had a bad fight with his mom. If he has, you may want to excuse him and let your playwright read in his place. Or maybe he has a legitimate complaint about another actor. Or even about you. Listen, see what you think, and do what you can, but if it's something very serious, Ms. Finney and I will help. That's our job. To help you do your job. We are the producers."

"So you got all the money," said Hector, and the others laughed.

"Right," I said. "No, actually, the director runs the rehearsals, but the producer is finally responsible for everything that happens. So, for example, you will work with the technical director on the set, costumes, props, etc. But I will arrange your meetings with them. Just as I may arrange meetings with adult volunteers, like this meeting we're having."

I could see a wave of relief roll across their side of the room and I realized I should have made this point sooner. Being the boss is one thing. Being responsible is another.

Next we plunged into "blocking," a theatrical word that simply means moving. Whether an actor goes down on one knee or walks all the way across the stage, the movement is called "blocking."

In order to map out the idea, I wrote on the board:

UR	UC	UL
DR	DC	DL

"U" stood for upstage, "D" for downstage, "R" for right, "L" for left, and "C" for center. The letters on the board represented a stage, I explained. Moving downstage meant moving closer to the audience and moving upstage away from it. Right and left were from the point of view of the actor, not the audience. Center, of course, was the center.

To clarify these terms, I had Jasmine get in front of the "audience" and had the other directors tell her to go "down right" or "up left" or wherever they wanted her to go. Soon they all had a good sense of the language.

"But why move?" I asked.

"So it won't be boring," said Monique.

"That's true. And what else? What does movement tell us?"

There were no answers, so I had Jasmine say the line "I love you" three ways: standing still, then with her back turned, and then moving away. Finally, she said the same line moving towards the audience.

"Does her movement change the meaning of those words?" I asked, and my point became clear.

Monique immediately sensed how she could strengthen a scene in Maria Margarita's play by having a line delivered with the daughter going down on one knee as she talked to the mother. It was a rather predictable choice, but she had understood and I praised her for it. At the same time, I urged the directors to let their actors explore before "setting" any movement.

"When you start your rehearsal, let the actors move as they feel. Some may stand ramrod still. Others may move hysterically around the stage. But if you first let them move as they want, they may discover an exciting way to emphasize a line—and it also makes them feel good about their work. It's another way to motivate."

"Yeah, another way to trick them," said Hector with a gleam.

"Yeah," said Clarence.

The girls also seemed to be meditating on their new power, and I realized that I might be creating monsters. Maybe my whole approach was wrong: I had started with logistics rather than objectives. I backtracked to my standard approach. "Why?" I heard myself saying.

"Why what?" asked Kim, sensing something was wrong.

"Why motivate them?"

"So they'll do it," said Hector, really getting into his role as the boss.

"But *why* do it?" I said with excessive intensity.

"So the play will work . . . ?" said Monique tentatively. She, too, sensed I felt uncomfortable.

"And why are we doing the play?" There was no response. The kids had settled into quiet. "Remember that first day," I said. "What did I talk about?"

"About our feelings and sharing them with others," said Kim.

I was startled. She had said exactly what I had hoped for.

After a moment's silence during which I marveled at Kim, wondered what Cliff would think of all this, and gathered courage, I went on. "Well, I betrayed that just now. I urged you to 'trick' the actors."

Jasmine leaned forward and said, "You mean when we're working with the actors, we're supposed to bring out their feelings — not trick them."

"Yes. If we start 'tricking,' we might as well quit right now. Now, many directors do just that. Because they have power and they start thinking the way I just did. But I want you to be directors who bring out the actors' feelings *because they are important* and the writer's play *because it's important.* And in doing that you will express yourself. Which will make it not just a good performance but a great one."

Clarence said, "And we won't lose in the quarterfinals."

The others didn't understand, so I had Clarence explain about his play in which a coach bullies boys into playing well but when they get close to winning, the kids make mistakes and lose — because they feel it was the coach's game, not theirs. It took Clarence a few minutes to articulate this, but the others stayed with him, especially when Cliff asked him questions.

At that point the first period bell rang, but I decided to keep them over. The meeting had been powerful and I wanted to reinforce it. But how? Part of me wanted to have them take an oath, but I quickly dismissed that and asked if they would mind meeting every week at this time, so we could discuss how it was going with the actors and technical directors.

Hector, who had been unusually quiet since his last remark about controlling the actors, said, "And we can keep each other from 'tricking.'"

The other kids seemed as surprised at Hector as I was, so it fell upon Hector to say finally, "So we're going to meet at this time every week?" To which everybody agreed. Cliff also volunteered to come.

In class later that day I explained blocking to the whole class and tried to emphasize the points about upstage and downstage by demonstrating "upstaging."

I brought Yalmilka and William (whose work, especially his acting, had been excellent ever since I praised his snake character) to the front and asked them to improvise a scene in which William wanted to punish Yalmilka and she wanted to run away. But I whispered in Yalmilka's ear the following instruction: always stay upstage of him. It took a few moments for Yalmilka to understand, but when she did she always moved away from the audience, and in doing so, forced William to turn his back to it. He was turned away from his audience almost the entire time. She had upstaged him, I explained. The kids got it.

I also used the opportunity to drive home the essential rule of staging: don't turn your back to the audience. If you do, your lines won't be heard and the nuances of expression will be lost.

Felix pointed out how there were occasions when turning away from the audience was essential, and I added, "Make those moments brief and try to say your line when you're facing out. That's the second most important rule I've given you. Who can remember the first?"

Hector, the new star student, yelled out, "Trust your feelings!"

"Right," I said. "When you're working today, try different ways of saying the lines, try different blocking. But always see if it feels right. If you're honest with your director, you can make the show not just good but brilliant."

At that point, we broke up into groups and they experimented with the plays.

Ms. Finney noticed the change in Hector. He had "found his calling."

"By a twist of fate," I said. I explained about the "tricking" incident.

Ms. Finney said, "Well, it sounds like you 'used' it," and we smiled at one another. "And Cliff too. He worked well. The question now is whether or not we want Kim to fill in for Alberto. It turns out he may be leaving for Puerto Rico."

"What's your feeling?" I said, stalling.

"I liked her as director. I think the other kids did too. And they like her play. She's winning respect. I have a hunch she'll make friends."

"We're being unfair all over the place."

"No, the rule is the writer takes over when somebody is sick."

"I guess I'm still reverberating from the meeting with Monique."

"Maybe you've taken on too much."

"And these directors' meetings on top of the others, but I didn't see how. . . ."

Ms. Finney looked at me and said, "Let Cliff run the meetings."

"Alone?"

"I'm here organizing in the room at that time. I'll just do my thing and keep an eye on them."

"I don't want you to burn out."

"That's a danger for you. Not me," she said.

I liked Ms. Finney's solution. The job would give Cliff a specific focus, and I felt he would be terrific with the directors. His seriousness—his priorities—had affected me. Or had I used him as a mirror? I definitely like to see myself reflected in the responses of young people such as Cliff. They seem to have fewer ulterior motives. They also can see the kids' point of view easier. They help me to keep on track. Either way, I liked having Cliff around.

I had to alert him to the dangers in the group: Hector reverting to "tricking"; Monique becoming hostile again; Clarence becoming his athletic coach; Jasmine's tentativeness—her shying away from conflict; Kim's fear of being an outsider. But even as I thought of those possibilities, part of me dismissed them as baggage. During the playwriting and now the directing, these kids had learned to express themselves directly. And that expression—Kim's play, Hector's call for the weekly meetings, Clarence's analogy to his sports career, Monique's ideas for directing, Jasmine's sensitivity to me—had led to action. These expressions made the kids feel better about themselves and would foster more directness, more action, and more self-respect.

As Cliff and I made our way to La Taza de Azul, I told him what I had been thinking. I also discussed four student directors I had worked with in the past: Michael and Emily, two junior high directors from Atlanta; Glen, an eighth grader from Brooklyn; and Iris, a seventeen-year-old from East Side High in Manhattan. Each discovered his or her own special talent as a director: Michael, an uncanny ability to relax actors, listening patiently to their complaints; Emily, the peripheral vision to keep various parts of the production — set, costumes, lights, actors — all working at the same time; Glen, stage business and prop invention; Iris, movements that reveal character. As different as they were in socio-economic background and age, they all responded to the director's role and found a new part of themselves.

I explained to Carmen how Cliff had started working because of the upcoming big production. "I never had anything like this growing up," she said as she made an espresso for a customer at the other end of the counter. "I want Venus to get as much as she can."

She also had an idea about costumes. William's mom had been a seam-stress who had worked for a fashion shop in Panama, but in the U.S. had eked out a living as a garment worker — until she collapsed of ner-vous exhaustion. Now on welfare, she had extra time and Carmen felt she would make splendid costumes, if we could give her a little money for materials. Carmen also assured me that she, Carmen, would go with William's mom to do the buying.

Cliff and I talked about his role as advisor to the directors, until Car-men served a wonderful roast chicken dish with garlic sauce, yellow rice, and red beans.

LISTENING

"Now," I said to the whole class, after Yalmilka had led an exercise routine she had seen on TV, "who can tell me how we began our improvs?"

"You sent me out of the room," said Felix.

"And after that?"

"You told him what to do," said Yalmilka, standing by her seat. The excitement of leading the exercises seemed to preclude sitting down.

"I did what?" I asked in mock horror. "I told an actor what to do? Shoot me, shoot me right now. No good director tells an actor what to do."

That brought Felix and Yalmilka up short, but not Luz. "He told Hector what he *wanted*," she explained.

"Right, and then he went for it. He 'does it.' Remember, directors. You can help to focus the wanting, but the actors do it."

"Now, the question for today is 'How does an actor do it?' Elizabeth, let's start with you. Let's do that section where your character wants to get her father to notice her new dress."

Moving with her dancer's grace, Elizabeth walked to the center of the room and said, in a coy, sweet voice, "Daddy, do you notice anything different?"

When I asked what happened, Maria Margarita said, "She spoke the lines," and Monique quickly added, "But she used them to get over on him."

"Good, now get him to notice *without* words," I said. Elizabeth came in primping and strutting. When I asked the kids what she was doing, what's she using to get him to notice, the shouted answer was "blocking."

When I asked Elizabeth to get the father's attention in a third way, I realized I hadn't talked to the class about "business," and quickly explained that "business" is the handling of props. Elizabeth looked confused, so I asked for suggestions from the floor and Yalmilka said, "Hand him his glasses." Elizabeth handed him a pair of imaginary glasses with a small flourish and everybody laughed. It had worked.

"So actors use three things — the lines, the blocking, and business — to get what they want. But even when they use all three to get what they want, they can be uninteresting. Does anybody know why?"

Nobody did, so I went on. "Good actors listen. Many people can look pretty or speak beautifully. Anybody can want and go for that wanting with the lines, the blocking, and business. But if you don't listen, you're going to commit the greatest sin an actor can commit: you're going to bore the audience."

"Everybody listens," said Elizabeth, who clearly felt she was on top of her craft and didn't know what I could be talking about.

"Do they? Think about your parents. Do they really listen to what you have to say? What about your little sister?"

"What about teachers?" demanded Felix.

"Right," I said. "We're human too. Questions? Problems? What am I not hearing? What is Ms. Finney not hearing? What is Cliff not hearing?"

"Cliff hears good," said Clarence. The other directors murmured approval.

After a short gripe session, in which the kids seemed to be trying on the act of complaining — the way one might try on a new, exotic style of clothes — I decided to set up an improv. Venus, who had been steadily stronger and more assertive (was it support from Carmen?) and William, who had been consistently strong as an improvisor, played student and teacher. William wanted the homework turned in without excuses. Venus wanted to explain why it couldn't be.

At first they stuck to their wanting. William said, "No excuses," and Venus said, "It's my little brother, he spilled catsup all over it." William again said, "No excuses" and the improv went on from there.

After a while, I brought it back to the lines above and asked William to respond differently to the spilled catsup line. "Whatever it makes you feel, just say it."

William proceeded to call Venus a liar, which enraged her, and the scene really took off. When I stopped it, there were protests, and everybody agreed it had been compelling.

"But *he* got to say what he wanted," pointed out Felix. "We gotta go by the script."

I asked William to do the same scene but limit himself to the line, "No excuses." He did, but managed to call her a liar with those two words and the scene was just as riveting. When the kids wanted to know why, I said because he listened. "As actors you have to listen, and if you do, your reactions will be true and powerful. And never boring."

Saul, who not only worked as the lighting designer, but also had one long speech as a fill-in actor in Jaime's play, had heard enough about listening. "How do you memorize?" he wanted to know.

"First, read the lines slowly, making sure you understand what the character's saying and how he or she feels about it—and why he or she is saying it right now. If you really understand in the beginning, it cuts the memorizing time in half."

"But I do understand and I can't."

"Next, read it with another actor, and listen to the other character's lines that come before and after. If you understand what they say and *why* they say it, that makes memorizing easier, too."

"Why, why, why—you always say 'why,'" sung out Kim. This observation had burst out of her as spontaneously as a jazz riff. I could sense Ms. Finney's pleasure.

"Yes, that's my theme song." And then, unable to resist, I said, "And why is that? What has it got to do with feelings? What happens when we ask 'why'?"

"We understand our feelings," said Monique. She said it without an edge.

"Or in this case we understand the character's feelings and then it's easier to remember what he or she says."

"But . . .," sputtered Saul.

"Then, you have to break up the speech. Divide it into parts. And then start with the first. Keep repeating it till you're sure of it—and always remembering why you're saying it—what the words mean. And then move on. When you have two sentences, start again from the beginning, doing both."

Deana, who had been cast in Kim's play, even though she had been absent quite a bit, asked what she could do if she started to giggle. Other kids made sympathetic noises. Clearly, they also saw giggling as a problem.

"There are two things to do: first you can prevent it by what? What makes an actor interesting—not boring?"

"Listening," came the answer from all over the room.

"Right, if you're really listening to the other actor, there won't be time to giggle."

"But what if you do, anyway?" asked Deana, who looked more confused than helped by the notion of listening.

"If you do, you 'go with it.' You make the character laugh, not you. You transform—remember that word; you change the meaning of—the laugh. It becomes part of the show, not an interruption of it."

To illustrate my point I had Deana come forward and say the first line of her part, "Cindy's a pain." As if on cue, she giggled.

"Good," I said. "If you giggle and say 'Cindy's a pain,' you can make it seem as if your character feels really devilish. Or she's embarrassed to be so mean. Either way works. Try it."

Deana went with "devilish" and everybody applauded. She had transformed the laugh from a negative to a positive. "You must stay in character," I concluded. "We never 'break character' by giggling, waving to friends in the audience, or stopping to comment on the character."

At that point, Ms. Finney had a question: "How do they learn to speak up, to be heard in a theater?"

"We already know one way. What do we do on stage, so we can be heard?"

"Face the audience—don't turn your back," said Clarence.

"Right. And another thing everybody can do, you can go up on the roof or somewhere nobody can hear you. Once you're there, go through your whole part *shouting*. That will loosen you up and when you come back you'll be loud enough on stage."

The answer to the next question in that session pleased me enormously. Anna, a girl who had been struggling throughout the course, asked, "What happens if you get nervous?"

"You do this," said Felix. He got up and started doing the first yoga breathing exercise.

"Yes, now let's all do it and then let's work on our scenes," I said. The kids began yoga breathing to Felix's rhythm.

I asked Ms. Finney if we had been in some kind of telepathic communication when Kim blossomed, when the sureness of her style finally matched the correctness of her answers. When Ms. Finney said yes, I went on to ask—rhetorically, really—if didn't she agree that we had come a long way from the time when it seemed I wanted the kids to reject the mind and concentrate only on the body, senses, and feelings.

"Feeling pretty cocky, aren't we?" said Ms. Finney, not unsympathetically, but I felt a little taken aback. "You have to remember," she continued, "these high moments can be followed by disasters. Remember we've already lost Alberto. It's fine that Kim has filled in as director. She's flourishing. But what happens when Kim's father beats her mother and her mother moves and. . . ."

What Ms. Finney said made chilling sense. When I had done shows in other poor neighborhoods, dropping out, sickness, and absenteeism had threatened weeks and weeks of good work. We had struggled through, of course, but I asked Ms. Finney if she had any ideas to counter these potential problems.

"Maybe the crew could be a second line of understudies. They could become familiar with all the parts in their unit, like the writers," said Ms. Finney, sounding like a seasoned off-off-Broadway producer.

"Yes, even if they don't memorize the lines, they could go out there, script in hand, and make it work."

"And we've got to make expectations clear. Like when we take class trips, the kids have to pay a quarter. When it was free, many simply wouldn't come. If nothing's expected of them, they just forget."

"That's what the contract does," I said. "We should bring it out again."

"And pray," said Ms. Finney.

Alone, I realized Ms. Finney's "realism" and my own "optimism" served as component parts of a greater process: the making of that living being, a show. What brings a show to life? Nobody really knows, but if everybody believes in a show and takes responsibility, the chances that it will work are immeasurably greater. Ms. Finney's thoughts about dropouts provided a case in point. She believed in the show but she also thought ahead. Of course there could be worse problems than dropouts. But even if the most catastrophic events happen, they can be overcome—if there is belief and responsibility. They are the grease that makes the individual parts mesh properly.

The producer must build that belief and responsibility. If he nurtures these feelings from the beginning, his co-workers anticipate and solve problems ahead of him. But if the producer takes all the responsibility and everybody else feels they are his dependent underlings, he reduces his options. He limits himself to his own imagination.

This notion made me think about our big show in Macon. We had committed ourselves to the kids' writing not only the script but the musical numbers. Then the music teacher decided the kids couldn't write music and didn't even bother to show up for the first writing session. The kids designated as songwriters milled around and finally became boisterous.

As producer I had to find a solution, but before the end of the day the puppetry teacher, who had seen the kids milling about, said she had a friend, a singer in clubs who wrote her own songs. The puppetry teacher would call the singer. Which she did. And the new young woman captured the imagination of the songwriters so successfully that everybody agreed afterwards the songs, especially the music written by a fourteen-year-old boy, had sparked the show.

Was it by chance that the puppetry teacher found the songwriting teacher for us? Partly. But as producer I had made a special effort to get extra papier-mâché supplies for the puppetry teacher. I also had helped make a time arrangement to cover her babysitting situation. And we had become friendly in the course of the various negotiations. So, when she called the songwriter, she urged her to come immediately and work for no pay. And the songwriter came.

When a producer gives his artists supplies and psychological support, art can thrive. Those little details make the difference between a show's being just "well acted" and the audience's feeling truly excited, between an exercise and magic.

On the way home I stopped at La Taza de Azul. I sat at my favorite seat, but instead of thinking I looked out the window. After a while Carmen came over.

"Are you OK?" she asked.

"Sure, just a little tired."

"Sometimes it's good not to think so much," she said.

"Yeah."

"I'll make you a cup," she said. She also made one for herself and sat down.

Sitting there and chatting with Carmen as the warm light of the spring afternoon streamed through the window, I felt whole, solid. I had faith in the kids, the production, the neighborhood—life.

19.

BACKSTAGE

I looked forward to my first meeting with the technical directors. The five — Saul, Victor, Benny, Maria, and Dawn — had been among the least successful writers and actors, but I felt this would be their chance.

My confidence came not only from my experience in doing shows, but also from their respective queries. Saul had asked about running lights. Benny and Victor had said they wanted to build sets together. Maria and Dawn had asked separately about costumes and make-up.

So my mission in that first meeting was not to interest them but to make them realize the importance and seriousness of their work. As it turned out, they—with Cliff's help—taught me how to reorganize our backstage world.

"You are going to do at least six jobs," I told the technical directors when they had gathered with Cliff and me in the empty classroom during lunch, "set designer, lighting designer, costume designer, make-up designer, prop master, and stagehand."

"What do you mean 'designer'?" asked Dawn, a heavy, dark-skinned girl.

"Well, the actors can't just go up on the stage. Somebody has to decide what's up there: is there a couch in the room? Is it a fancy room or a run-down one? Where are the doors? What's the whole layout? And somebody also has to decide about the lights: when the lights come on; how bright they will be; what colored gels to use and—and *why*. And the actors can't just wear any old clothes. Their clothes must be right for their character. Somebody has to coordinate that. The same goes for make-up."

"That ain't gonna be us," said Victor, sensing my thrust.

"Oh yes. Each one of you is going to design all parts of your show. And when we do it, you're all going to help each other make that design work. So, for example, Saul, you have Jaime's play. You have to design the set but you can't move all the furniture, get the props ready, run the lights, and pull the curtain. You have to assign one of your buddies here to do those jobs."

"But I want to do lights."

"Right, but what about all the other jobs? You can't rely on the actors to pull the curtain, move the furniture, and get the props ready."

"They should do the props," said Benny.

"No, you're going to do it all. This crew right here. If we let all the actors do what they want backstage, it will be chaos. You have to be in charge."

"I thought the director was the boss," said Victor, even more uneasy.

"Not backstage. He watches the show out front. To see what the actors are doing."

"I just want to do make-up," said Dawn.

"You can do make-up, but you also have to do all these other jobs," I said, looking at five sullen faces.

Maria said, "Why can't I just do costumes and Dawn the make-up?"

"And me the lights," said the persistent Saul.

"And me and Victor building things," said Benny.

"Because I want you to learn all the different trades. You will each have a notebook with five sections, and in each section you have one trade: set, lights, props, make-up, and costumes. But they all will relate to one show. You'll only have to learn one show. You'll be part of that show. Many important parts."

"Ah, could I suggest something here?" asked Cliff. He wore a Chuck Berry tee shirt that day but his manner was tentative and respectful. "What might be interesting would be Dawn learning all five shows by doing make-up for all of them."

"But that way they won't be exposed to as many crafts."

"Well, they might learn the one craft really well," said Cliff. "That's what the actors and directors are doing."

"But they wouldn't be part of one show. They'd miss the fun of teamwork."

"They'd have each other, the other crew members. That would be their home base," said Cliff. His manner remained respectful but seemed firmer.

The kids hung on every word of this debate, and when I heard myself say, "It's always worked well this way," the words sounded lame. Which made me—finally—turn to the kids and ask them what they felt.

They became mute. Taking sides against an adult suddenly had little appeal to them. Finally it took a secret ballot to make Cliff's idea policy. Unanimously.

We concluded the meeting by arranging to get copies of all five scripts to all five technical directors. They would read them for the next meeting. They also each had to get a notebook with five dividers in it. One divider for each show, not each trade.

At the next session it was agreed that Benny would be nominally in charge of props and Victor the sets, but they would work together. Benny would make a prop list for each show in his book. Victor would start with a ground plan for each in his. Meanwhile, Dawn started on make-up for each character in each of the plays, and Maria on their costumes. Saul would design the lighting.

Before they began, I emphasized that their designs should be more than pretty pictures. They had to reflect the plays. If Kim's play is about a family bursting apart, the colors in the costumes should be bright, wild—violent. So should the colors in the make-up. The set could be crowded, ready to split. The lights had to be bright, harsh.

The kids took all this in and then Dawn quietly raised her hand. "But the little girl isn't violent. It's them. The parents."

"So she shouldn't have such bright make-up?"

"Yeah," she said as if she were talking to a particularly dull little brother.

"Yes. Every character is different. And that would go for the clothes, too, Maria."

Maria nodded tolerantly, two steps ahead of me.

The designers worked intensely all lunch hour as Cliff and I circulated, responding to their drawings.

At the next rehearsal, the designers moved from play to play watching the actors and directors, getting a better sense of the shows, and making notes for revising the designs.

When they completed revisions, I took them to the stage in the auditorium and we walked around backstage, noting the lighting board (really just switches on the wall), the curtain, an area for the prop table, the section where we could keep set pieces, and the space for actors to dress (which was nil).

"Now," I said. "It's time to get realistic. We're going to talk about time. There are five plays. Most of those plays have more than one scene. One has four. That's at least ten breaks for the audience to sit through. The audience, as you know, will include kindergarten children as well as sixth graders. They can only sit a limited amount of time. Who can tell me what I'm getting at?"

"We can't spend all day on set changes," said Saul.

"What does that mean?" snapped Benny.

"It means," said Maria, "you guys can't have two couches and a love seat, plus a refrigerator and a kitchen table like you got in Maria Margarita's play."

"But it's that kind of apartment," said Victor. "A real family apartment. So when the divorce —"

"They won't even remember there was a divorce in the first scene, if they have to wait for you guys to move all that stuff," said Dawn.

"We can move it twice as fast as those actors could change into the second bunch of costumes Maria's got for them," said Benny.

"Just the walk down the hall to the bathroom is gonna take five minutes," said Victor.

Cliff started to intervene but I waved him off. I wanted the bloodletting to happen now. After it was over, they would all redesign their work. There simply wasn't time or facilities for heavy, realistic sets or costumes. We had to "suggest" them.

It took the kids a while, but they got the notion of "suggestion." One chair draped with a dark fabric and a couple of pillows could suggest a room full of heavy pieces; a scarf or sunglasses a change of clothes.

The kids revised their drawings a third time, but I wasn't sure how they felt about the changes until they presented them to the directors at one of the early morning directors' meetings.

Cliff had prepared the directors on the notion of suggestion, but the two groups still saw the designs from different perspectives. The directors were not only the "bosses on the set," they were the top students and, except for Kim, members of the socially in-crowd. The designers were neither.

The structure of the meeting also seemed to favor the directors. They sat in different sections of the room and the designers moved with designs to each of them — a bit like traveling salespeople. But these salespeople, having been forced to think through, revise, and revise again, knew their wares. As Cliff and I circulated, I heard the designers speaking with real authority.

For example, Saul said, "The lights have to go out one at a time," to Monique, who had said she wanted a blackout. "Look," he continued, "if Veronica has just heard her parents are splitting, the audience should see how she feels. And, if you have her walk in front of the curtain, with the spot following her, it will give the others more time to change the set and costumes." But Monique felt her actress couldn't sustain the moment; it would become phony. "Then give her some business," suggested Saul. "Have her hug her teddy bear or something."

Maria told Hector that there was no need for a costume change in Jaime's play, except the script said the second scene was the next day.

"Well what do you want me to do?" said Hector.

"Talk to the *writer*, have him change the script to 'later the same day,'" whispered Maria.

"I'll take care of that," said Hector.

Even Benny was able to tell Jasmine that the child didn't need an entire rock collection as props when he was in his room alone. "He can have his *favorite* rock," he explained. "The rest is *suggested.*"

Discussions with the individual actors about costume and make-up proved less successful. In almost every case, the director and even Ms. Finney, Cliff, or I had to intervene. But, as I explained to the designers, such fights are inevitable. Arguments occur in the professional theater all the time. "The actor wants to look a certain way. And he or she is the one out there onstage," I explained. "But even so, you must stand up for your choices. And even if you compromise, you can make your point."

On cue Felix came over to complain about wearing a sports shirt. He wanted to wear a white shirt and tie. It would make him look older, he declared. Maria and I looked at each other and then she proceeded to explain that the character was a jazz musician, not a banker.

Some parents helped with costumes. Others had to be coaxed by Carmen. Still others, like William's mom, had their own ideas and often tried to improve the kids' designs. That drew ire from the designers and their parents—not to mention the actors.

Similar excesses of enthusiasm almost destroyed the mural that was to be a backdrop for Jaime's play and the cardboard "sandwich" signs for the computers in Luis's play. The mural got ripped when four kids worked on it at once. And six kids fought for the privilege of painting the signboard during one work session at lunch. Maria finally restricted the painting crew to Benny and Victor.

Still, when the actors began wearing the costumes, and the make-up and sets and props appeared, the designers knew they had done something quite remarkable.

Ms. Finney, who had been dealing with parents on the costume crisis, said, "'SUGGEST' will be written on my gravestone." She had had to urge the parents to restrain their desire to "decorate" the costumes. But she also went on to reveal to me how much she had learned (I had thought she knew all anybody could) about the various families. She learned that Jasmine's mother was a single parent working as a bank teller. The bank had a branch in the neighborhood but denied Jasmine's mother's repeated requests for transfers there. So Jasmine's mother traveled three hours a day, worked eight hours, took care of three children, cooked, cleaned, and shopped without a husband or child support.

Ms. Finney also felt optimistic about the designers. All their schoolwork had improved, she said. "In a way, this has been the most successful part."

Oddly, I felt sad. It may have been Ms. Finney's revelations about the various families, but I was thinking of what would happen to Saul and the others in junior high and after. Would this success have any lasting impact? Would any of them have anything to do with the theater again? Maybe some of the kids like Luz, Kim, and Maria Margarita might, but not the Saul's and the Maria's. And I couldn't help thinking I might be raising expectations in a context of hopelessness.

When I confessed my feelings, Ms. Finney said, "That's what a teacher has to ask every day."

"And the answer?"

"There are individual moments, individual cases—we're not changing the world here."

"So why do you do it?"

"Why do *you* do it?" Ms. Finney countered.

"To satisfy my do-gooder side, I guess. If I look at it objectively, my work—it's all very active but what does it accomplish? I'd be better off doing something political. Or spending my time writing about the conditions here."

Ms. Finney looked at me a moment and then said, "I have an uncle. He was a successful teacher in Ireland. At the same time he worked for the IRA—until he felt he could do more for Ireland by quitting the teaching and coming to America to fundraise. He's been miserably lonely and not very effective here."

"But politics is important."

"This man is a teacher. His contribution was as a teacher. I think he was ashamed of his success."

"That's psychiatric nonsense," I said too sharply.

"The man is a teacher. And so are you. For both of you it's a calling."

"But if it's futile. . . ."

"Why don't you just teach, be with the children—and let the arm-chair philosophers write letters to the editor."

Ms. Finney's eloquence ended the discussion, but not my thoughts as I left P.S. 34 on that clear, warm spring day. She was right, as far as she went. But why did my teaching have to be limited to twenty sessions with a group? Why not teach more of what I know, why not take the kids further? That didn't have to mean their going into show-biz. Or even a real interest in the theater. But if children dealt with artistic problems on an on-going basis, they would develop a special approach to life's problems. They would gain an artistic point of view.

The weather seemed so promising I decided to pass up *cafe con leche* and walk to Third Avenue, the next subway stop back to Manhattan. Walking down 138th Street, I enjoyed the hopefulness of the bridal shops and Kiddie stores, even as I sensed the desperation of the check cashing storefronts and rundown *bodegas*. Life seemed to renew itself, regardless of the difficulties, that fine spring day.

But what about me? Even if I became a classroom teacher, the kids would spend only forty weeks with me. I wanted more time than that.

I really wanted to work with them for years. I wanted to spend time with them the way my coach, Louis, spent time with me and the other kids who hung around Poinsettia Park in Los Angeles where I grew up. Louis coached us in football, baseball, basketball, track, and in various "All Around" competitions, which included tennis, "sea war," caroms, and other diversions provided by the L.A. City Department of Recreation and Parks.

As I thought about it, all those sports were really incidental. The contact with Louis and the rest of the older guys mattered more. We took them as role models, and grew to face the world as they faced it.

The 52nd Street Project in New York provides the same kind of experience, I decided as I went down the subway steps. The plays and the classes stimulate the kids, but the intimate contact between kids and adults matters more.

Both of those experiences took place after school, I realized, on the #6 train coming back downtown. I needed to see the kids every day after school from age seven to seventeen. I really wanted to become part of the neighborhood. To start my own after-school center there.

Yes. What if I worked with a Luz or a Kim every day for ten years? Or a Saul or a Felix? Or what about Candy from Stilson, Georgia? Or Amy and Geneva from Atlanta? Whatever else happened, they would look at the world with an artist's eyes.

20.

GETTING READY

The rehearsals took place in bits and pieces over a five-week period (professionals in the USA get three weeks, eight hours a day; in European and Eastern European countries they get twelve weeks), and had many highs and lows.

At the beginning of each session, I made a brief, "state-of-the-production" speech. I would emphasize how little time we had, what the problems in the previous day's rehearsal were, and what we should work on that day. But mostly I played cheerleader: I announced that Felix had begun to listen, that Luz now knew her lines letter-perfect, that a wonderful chemistry had been developed between the crew members, etc.

The individual rehearsals, of course, varied, but we followed a standard procedure: 1) break down the script (divide it into small sections); 2) work a small section (experiment with different approaches to lines, blocking, and business); 3) set the blocking and business for that section; 4) memorize the lines, blocking, and business at home; 5) run the lines from the previous session (test the actors' memory for the words without trying to act them); 6) do the scene on its feet (act the whole section, integrating lines, blocking, and business) and move onto the next section, repeating the same techniques. When we had gone through the entire script like this, we added 7) props, 8) costumes, 9) the set, 10) run-throughs (acting the whole play without interruptions from the director, who gave "notes" or suggestions afterwards), 11) a technical rehearsal, 12) a dress rehearsal, and 13) three performances.

Reading and discussing had taken all of the first session. At the second we broke down the scripts. "Breaking down" a script means dividing it into its component beats. All of those divisions had been decided by the directors in their morning meetings. So the rest of the kids, all of whom had scripts (thanks to the computer department), took out pencils and marked the beats.

In the group doing Kim's play, the breakdown went quickly because she was both writer and director. But Jaime argued with Clarence's decision to make the first scene three beats instead of two. When I came over, I reminded Jaime that Clarence, the director, was in charge of the rehearsal, and then when Jaime told me he didn't care, I pulled him aside.

"It's my play. I wrote it," Jaime said when we were safely in the hall.

"But you can't cross the director in rehearsal. Talk to him *after*. But not in the middle."

"He's still wrong."

"That may be, but you've got to know when and how to correct him." Stoically, Jaime went back to the rehearsal.

Maria Margarita and Monique worked together. Monique suggested the starting point of the various beats, but then asked if Maria Margarita agreed. Maria Margarita responded openly and soon the actors also added their opinions. Finally, when everybody had a say, Monique decided and Maria Margarita and the others deferred.

Hector and Jasmine broke down the other two plays. Hector's style tended toward the autocratic and Jasmine's toward anti-heroic self-effacement. Both got the job done quite nicely.

"Working the beat" means the actors deliver their lines various ways. It's experimentation, and I urged the kids to start with wanting—"What does your character want? That will suggest where to move, how to say the lines"—but soon Felix and Deana in Kim's play began trying to do it in "opposite" ways, e.g., slow versus fast, loud versus soft, active versus quiet. And when I pointed out their technique to the rest of the group, others tried it. Tyrone and William, who were playing computers, for example, speeded up their lines and discovered an exaggerated style that later became the "computer strut," used throughout that play. But the classic example of working came from Venus and Yalmilka, the other two characters in Luz's play.

Venus played the dead grandmother who came to Yalmilka's character in dreams. Venus spoke the lines sweetly, kindly—as if the grandmother came straight from a Norman Rockwell illustration. But the scenes I had felt were the strongest in Luz's play never happened. Finally I asked Jasmine, the director, about the God character Monique had suggested in the human character improv. What had *he* been like?

"Cranky," answered Jasmine.

"Yes," I said. "Now, we don't always think of God as cranky. But it worked. Why don't you ask Venus to stop being such a nice grandma?"

Let her try it all kinds of ways."

Venus proceeded to play her role in a variety of un-grandma-like ways. What emerged was a crackling performance, at once angry, mercurial, devilish, and loving. Venus's character, in turn, inspired Yalmilka. This helped the two of them hold their own in the scenes with Luz.

As the working process can take days, I urged the directors to divide their rehearsals into time units and when the time (say, ten minutes for a half-page beat) ended, to set the blocking.

At first the directors felt they had to re-block everything differently from what the actors had worked, but when I assured them they could keep exactly what the actors had done (or modify it), the directors relaxed noticeably and the actors cooperated better.

Writing the blocking down proved to be a greater problem. I had written the following shorthand on the board:

X = cross or move across the stage
R = stage right
L = stage left
U = upstage
D = downstage

And gave the example of an actor moving downstage left to speak his line. In that case, the actor would write "X DL" on the page opposite the line (the blank back side of the previous page's dialogue).

The kids understood this new code but were impatient with making notes. They were sure they would remember how they moved. But I told the directors they would be responsible for each actor noting his or her blocking; that I would check the scripts. And I made a point to check Felix's script. He called that "discrimination." But kids, like adult actors, forget. Noting the blocking on paper helps the memory and prevents blocking errors later on.

At the beginning of the next session we did a "line-through" of the beats that had been "worked." That meant the actors put away the scripts and tried to recite their lines, without dramatizing them. This test-like emphasis on pure memory brought out various responses. Luz memorized the lines perfectly and wanted to recite her blocking (her director let her). Felix paraphrased everything, which irritated Kim, and I had to intervene. Deana remembered all her short lines but drew a blank if a speech was more than two sentences.

I rephrased my advice to Saul about memorizing and to that I added the suggestion that little sisters and brothers—even parents on some occasions—could often be enlisted to give cues. And once I repeated that there was no substitute for understanding your lines and repeating them over and over again.

After the line-through, the kids "ran" or did the previous day's work "on its feet"—going through the blocking and saying the words with meaning.

I watched Rosa and Anna run a scene from Maria Margarita's play. It had been a splendid scene when they were working on it, but now it dragged. I asked if they had noticed. They had. So had Monique, the director. I asked them why it dragged. They didn't know, but Maria Margarita, the long-suffering writer, did.

"They weren't listening to each other," she said.

"Yes," I agreed. "Now that you know the lines and blocking you really can start listening."

At first the kids mimed props, pouring imaginary milk from an imaginary carton into an imaginary glass and the like with varying degrees of conviction, but when the actors had lines—and the particular prop was ready—they integrated that prop with the lines and blocking. Benny cleared a table at the back and the actors picked up their props and returned them to the table before and after each rehearsal, checking them in and out on a sheet of paper he guarded tenaciously.

When we had reached the fourth rehearsal, all the plays had been blocked and memorized, so we tested them on the stage.

There were logistical problems. Other classes needed the auditorium. And I wasn't at school every day. Luckily, Ms. Finney arranged to use the auditorium for activities like free reading, and the various groups took turns trying out their blocking and lines on the stage while the others did free reading.

At the fifth rehearsal, I urged the kids to bring in their costumes and we did a disappointing run-through on the stage. The kids spoke too softly. Many forgot blocking. Some dropped lines. Even Luz's voice dropped a bit.

We had scheduled a technical rehearsal for the following Wednesday, but the lackluster work at the fifth made me feel we weren't ready, so I added two more early morning rehearsals. That meant being at school by 7 A.M., but the kids made it (with a couple of exceptions, and on those occasions the writers read in, carrying their own scripts).

At those morning rehearsals, I stood beside the regular director and in between his or her directions I found myself yelling "louder, louder, louder," in spite of my plan to let the directors handle everything. I also offered my services to work with particularly soft-spoken actors, calling them aside and asking them to remember why they were saying particular lines.

The most dramatic moment came when Hiram, who was playing a hood in Jaime's play, forgot a speech and stormed off the stage.

The others ran the scene with Jaime reading in and I pulled Hiram aside.

"I can't do it," he said.

"Of course you can."

"Look what I did. I just forgot. I'm loud, I'm louder than anybody, but. . . ."

"Hiram, that happens to professionals all the time. And you know what they do?" Hiram was staring at the floor. "They improvise. Just like we've done in class."

"But what about the cues?"

"Say what the character feels. The other actor will fit it in, or improvise with you. Just remember who your character is. You might forget the words but you know this guy. He's a punk. He doesn't believe anything or anybody. He distrusts everybody."

"They'll all think I'm stupid."

"No, they'll think you have the brains to think on your feet. They'll also think you have the guts to hang in there."

"Can't we have somebody to tell us the lines?"

I had decided against a prompter—I wanted the kids to improvise and we really didn't have an extra person—but sitting there with Hiram, sensing his anxiety, I realized how silly I had been. I said, "Sure," and I went to enlist Saul, whose competence and energy had made him the leader backstage.

I presented it as a promotion: Saul would stage-manage as well as run the lights. He would hold the scripts and have final say in any disputes backstage.

Saul said, "Great, I know most of the lines anyway."

Having the security of the stage manager "on book" and knowing that improvisation was acceptable made Hiram letter-perfect the rest of the rehearsals and at all the performances.

In the technical rehearsal, where we tried the props, lights, and set pieces together, we stumbled from one crisis to the next. The designers had worked out all the set changes on paper, but rushing around to move set pieces and props amid the actors, the tech crew bumped into each other, started yelling ("They seemed to project better than the actors," Ms. Finney informed me dryly), had temper tantrums, and made the actors even more nervous. Hector added another level of madness by rushing to the stage from his spot at the back of the auditorium, shouting that the refrigerator was off its mark.

When it was over, a discouraged and disgruntled company sat in the auditorium's first two rows. We would have a dress rehearsal the following Monday and the show on Wednesday! Disaster seemed certain. So I smiled.

"This," I said, "was a classic tech rehearsal. We made almost every mistake you can make. You know what that means?" I knew nobody would reply, so I answered myself. "It means we'll probably make the others in the dress rehearsal and then we'll knock their socks off in the show. I can just feel it."

My Pollyanna speech moved nobody. Luz spoke for the group when she said, "Can we have another rehearsal?"

My instinct would have been to let it go, but I agreed to come early on Monday so we could do two dress rehearsals.

In those sessions, good things began to happen: in some parts of a scene, actors remembered their blocking better and spoke louder, a set change moved quicker, the "wave" curtain call almost worked.

In my final instructions I told the actors, "Listen, listen, and listen some more. Enjoy each other. And if somebody drops a line, give them a chance to get it from Saul. But don't break character. Keep in character. *Live those characters.* The same with blocking. If somebody makes a mistake, work around it, just as you would in life. Walk over to them and lead them as your character might, if you have to. Do what you feel like, *as the character would.* And the same with the crew: if there's a mistake, just correct it and keep moving. If the actors stay in character, nobody will notice. And we'll have fun. Which is what we're here for. Let's have fun."

"Ideally what I should have done is let the directors alone," I said to Cliff and Ms. Finney as we sat in Kevin's, a bar across the street from the police station and only a couple of blocks from the school. Cliff had said the directors felt I had eclipsed them. They were right.

"I'm not criticizing," said Cliff. "You asked."

"I probably subverted the whole lesson."

"You did fine, you did fine," said Ms. Finney impatiently. "Besides, can you imagine what those kids would feel if their parents and the principal and people from the district couldn't hear them?"

"Not to mention their friends," said Cliff.

"Not to mention me," said Ms. Finney.

"I'll have a meeting with the directors," I said.

"First, you have to relax," said Ms. Finney as our beers arrived. She pushed a beer toward me.

After a pause, Ms. Finney said, "My husband thinks I'm crazy. I sit there watching TV and lecturing him about the actors 'listening.' Or 'telegraphing emotions.'"

"My thing is blocking," said Cliff. "I look at that stuff on TV and I see how it simply isn't motivated. It's all activity. No action."

I looked at them and said, "I just wish the kids—"

"Oh, shut up," said Ms. Finney.

We looked at each other and I said, " 'Shut up, is it?'"

Ms. Finney giggled and I giggled back. "Yes, 'shut up' it is. The kids are fine. It's us," she said. "And the district board. And Mr. Hyman."

"I've got to write a twenty-page paper on this production in"—Cliff looked at his watch—"twenty-two hours."

"Owwwwww. . .," I said and paused. "What we've got to remember is that the audience will inspire the kids—"

"The way they did in Macon. Or was it Atlanta?"

I got the distinct feeling Ms. Finney would be unreceptive to another "southern story." Even I wasn't really keen for one.

"What we have to do is prepare for a failure," she said. "You've got

to go out in front of that audience and talk about the learning 'process.'
And mistakes not being failure. You know: the whole nine yards."

"Yeah, and I could just tape that and transcribe it as my paper," said
Cliff, who would videotape the performance.

"Hello, Ms. Finney, Cliff—hello, Ms. Finney, Cliff—are you there?"
I said. They just looked at me. "They're not going to fail," I said.

"We don't *want* them to fail," said Ms. Finney. "Those are two different things."

"Oh, I don't know." It was all getting to me. "What if I do get up there
and blab about the 'process.'"

"The kids will probably kill you," said Cliff, who was on his second
beer. "But it might make things easier for Mr. Hyman."

"Oh, what's the difference," said Ms. Finney. "We can just skip town
tomorrow."

"Right," I said. I realized what was happening: our job was over. "It's
their show now, that's all. We have to let go," I said.

"Their show," said Ms. Finney as she raised her beer. So did Cliff and
I. We drank.

When I reached the subway, a clearly agitated Kim appeared; she had
been waiting for me. I whisked her to a nearby coffee shop.

She had a Coke and I drank coffee while she told me her father had
heard about the play.

"So he's coming?"

"I don't know."

"What about your mom?"

Kim shrugged.

Kim also revealed that her mother wanted her to withdraw the play.
"It could be dangerous," she had said to Kim. This despite the fact that
the mother had not read the play.

"Well, what do you want to do?"

"I want to do it," she said. "She won't come, and him—he probably
won't even know. I don't think he really knows."

"Could it really be dangerous? If he did know. If he did come."

"It's always dangerous," said Kim fiercely, but she thought it might be a good idea if I spoke to her mother.

Kim's mother, a black woman of forty with her hair braided into dreadlocks, wore shorts and a tee shirt that said DON'T WORRY BE HAPPY. Only a strained look in her eyes made her appear at all extraordinary.

We talked for half an hour. It was clear that she was a woman in distress, but also that she loved Kim. Eventually she admitted that her husband knew nothing of the production. She had felt Kim would humiliate her. But when we talked about the play, she responded. It turned out her husband played the saxophone; art was not a foreign language to either of them. Finally she said all would be fine. Kim seemed relieved.

At La Taza de Azul, Carmen reassured me too. "He sleeps downtown," she said. "Besides, he won't go to the school. Not him. He'll talk. That's all."

But the next day when I told Ms. Finney, she said, "We've got to tell Hyman." I was afraid she would say that, but there was nothing else to do.

In Mr. Hyman's office, I assured him the production was in good shape, and then said, "One girl was afraid her mother and father would be hurt by the portrait of them, but I reassured the mother."

"What about the father?"

"He hasn't lived there in a long time. He doesn't know about it."

"So you're confident there will be no problem. I don't want a fist fight in my auditorium."

"Nor do we want a fist fight back at their apartment," said Ms. Finney.

"I'll take responsibility," I said. "I talked to her. It's going to be very therapeutic," I said, grappling for a soothing word.

"Not if he feels he's been humiliated in public," said Ms. Finney.

"He's not going to show. But if he does, I'll handle him," I said.

"No you won't. I'm the principal," Mr. Hyman said and paused. "It's that good, the play?"

Both Ms. Finney and I nodded.

"And as far as you know, he doesn't even know about the production?"

"Right," I said, as I looked at Mr. Hyman and remembered seeing him after he had stopped a fight between parents in front of the school. The two women had scratched and kicked him as well as each other.

"So the odds are good. But let's improve them. We'll cancel the afternoon performance. That way he would have to come at 9 or 10:30. And be among all those little kids."

Hiding my disappointment, I said, "You won't be sorry." It could have been worse. Much worse.

That night I slept badly, fantasizing battles on stage and in the street. Everything was my fault. So I got up and thought about all the writers like Thomas Wolfe, who "hurt" their families.

I thought again about Kim's play. All of the characters cared about each other. That would come through, as would Kim's honesty and wisdom. And her love. But if the man decided to be offended, Kim could hardly defend herself. And I could walk away, leaving her with a man who might react violently.

Finally, I decided that if he was that crazy, he would find an excuse some other time. No matter what Kim or her mother did. Writing the play was an act of courage that might help liberate Kim. And if we cancelled the show now, she might become even more frightened of her father. Also, the odds were definitely in our favor. It was worth the risk.

21.

DOING IT

The cancellation of the afternoon performance jolted the kids. Felix suggested a strike, Hector called a special directors' meeting, and others, like Deana and Elizabeth, expressed their shock by becoming more and more jittery. But by the morning of the performances all energy focused on dressing the set, trying on costumes with make-up, and doing line-throughs.

At 8:30 that morning, the company gathered in the first two rows again, and I answered questions and responded to problems. We worked out the logistics of which performers waited where (there were no extra seats in the theater; the kids had to stay in their classroom until their show). I reminded them yet again about listening. And then we did relaxation exercises.

Our many exercise sessions vindicated themselves. The yoga breathing and the tension release exercises not only relaxed their bodies but provided a reassuring sense of familiarity. It helped focus the kids.

Kindergarten-third grade classes came to the first show. Ms. Finney had wondered about showing such young children the problems in Kim's and Maria Margarita's plays or the raw emotion in Luz's, but we decided they would like the live actors and happy endings. Besides, our plays were tame compared to what they saw on TV.

Luis's play about the computers immediately caught the fancy of the younger children. The actors had been warned to wait until the laughter subsided before delivering their next lines, so the show ran a bit long, but to a totally satisfied audience. And, for a few weeks that spring, the "computer strut," I was told later, became more popular than break-dancing.

Jaime's mystery play also was a hit. It appealed to the kids' sense of fun and thrills, even as it demanded that the audience understand how an older brother's loyalty to his family eclipsed his wish for money.

More surprisingly, the two serious plays seemed to find an audience. When Anna said "Your father and I are going to separate" in Maria Margarita's play, the 180 kids who had been roaring at the computer play sat still and quiet. And when Felix, as the father in Kim's play, started screaming, the kids winced and scrunched into their seats. The cheers at the reconciliations bespoke real catharsis.

But Luz's play provided the greatest surprise of the first show. I had considered it strong on feeling but unclear about the characters' motivations. The kids saw it differently: they responded to the dead grandmother, who in the dream sequences appears to Yalmilka's character, the little girl. What I had considered a play about betrayal and the importance of material things turned out to be a hymn to the extended family; the grandmother's character, played by the amazing Venus, and her role in the family—not the wisdom she dispensed—clearly carried the play's "message." Like the audience, I saw it freshly that morning.

The second audience, fourth through sixth graders, provided the ultimate test. Would they respond with giggles and sneers? Or talk throughout the whole thing? Would they be bored? Or could we reach them?

The company rose to the occasion. As soon as the curtain opened on Luz's play, Maria ran to the classroom to summon the cast of Jaime's play. Meanwhile, the crew readied the next scene change and Venus prepared to enter. As she entered in a half-light provided by the ubiquitous Saul, Luz exited and went behind a special curtain for a costume change. The kids executed these and most of the many other transitions crisply. As a result, set changes and cooperation between actors and crew backstage melded into a collective act. Each moment lived on its own, but a spirit suffused all of them. And that spirit inspired the actors, who gave wonderful performances.

The audience began partaking of the performances, and suddenly theater magic radiated throughout the auditorium, manifesting itself in the body language of fourth graders who seemed to do the computer strut along with William and Tyrone; in the voice of a fifth-grade girl who "talked back" to Luz, when she punished Yalmilka; in the cheers for the Big Brother when he stood up to the gangster in Jaime's play; in the quiet during the divorce scene in Maria Margarita's. And when the audience's response became more intense, the actors listened more closely, and moved with greater authority. Which, in turn, pulled the audience still further into the play. As we say in the theater, we "crossed over."

Special moments included:

—Felix crying after he embraced Elizabeth and Deana at the end of Kim's play: this was not in the script and had not been rehearsed. The tears simply emerged and pushed the already powerful scene two notches higher.

—Venus' authority on stage, as the grandmother: her development from the shy girl who did the first sound-and-motion to this full-blown performance had been steady and true. In retrospect it seemed inevitable that she would emerge a star.

—Luz and Yalmilka listening to each other: Luz's natural talent seemed to feed Yalmilka and give her a strength that made their scenes unforgettable.

—William and Tyrone doing the computer strut at their curtain call and some of the fourth-grade kids in the audience jumping up to do it in the aisles. Tyrone's uninhibited joy was so strong that even if he had fallen and dirtied his white pants, I was certain he would have kept "strutting."

—Deana, who initially had such trouble speaking loud enough, enunciating and projecting so she could be heard all the way in the back.

—Felix and Hector shaking hands with grudging respect after the show (oh, to have a photo of that!).

—Jaime's pride when he, the "dumb" one, took his curtain call as *author.*

—My encounter with Carmen after the show: I saw her first and threw my arms around her and yelled, "She's a star!"

"No thanks to me," Carmen said, and when I looked at her questioningly, she added, "I gave her hell this morning."

"She probably deserved it."

"But before the show?"

"She knows you believed in the show—who did more?. . ."

"I'm so proud," she said.

"Justifiably," I said, and we laughed.

But looking over her shoulder, I saw a short white man talking intensely to Felix. Next to the man was Kim's mom. The man could be only one person. Kim had disappeared.

I walked over and introduced myself to Kim's father. To my great relief, he waxed eloquent about the show. As did Kim's mom. But I quickly realized they had not been transformed by Kim's art, they were simply reinterpreting it. In effect, he was justifying himself and she was acquiescing. He also assured me that he was going to manage Kim's career. Make her a lot of money. . . .

Would that be a lesson for Kim? That question plagued me as I accepted the congratulations of other parents, Mr. Hyman, and a woman from the local school board. We had a hit, but what about Kim?

Back in the classroom, I found her talking with Maria Margarita and Monique. They seemed animated, a group of friends. I hated to interrupt.

Kim would have preferred to stay with her friends, but she agreed to talk. What had she felt about her father and mother's coming?

"I don't know—nuthin'. The same," she said.

"How do you feel about the play?"

"Five kids have told me their families are just like that! They wanted to know how I knew about them, and the applause. . . ." There was wonder and pride in her voice.

That response validated the whole experience for me. I was only too happy to release Kim to her new friends. The play hadn't changed her parents, but Kim had not only grown and found a place among her peers but also gotten a sense of the power and joy of writing.

Lunch hour approached, but nobody wanted to go. It seemed necessary to discuss each detail of the show. Ms. Finney and I finally moved the post mortem to the lunchroom, where the company was greeted with cheers by the rest of the fifth and sixth grades.

In the teachers' lunch room, Ms. Finney, Cliff, and I enjoyed the congratulations, but I think all three of us would have preferred to be with the kids.

It would have been difficult to top the full production under ideal conditions, so I called Ms. Finney later in the week and suggested we quit while we were still ahead. But she remained firm: each child should have a play done, one way or another.

As Ms. Finney, Cliff, and I cast roles for the first radio broadcast, I anticipated a let-down, and when we broke up into the old play units, confusion did, in fact, ensue.

Ms. Finney created order by calling the kids back to their seats and reminding them that each writer deserved the best production possible. Next, she re-read the original cast list, which had indicated not only what people did in the full production but also whose plays would be done as radio plays, whose as video, whose as staged readings. The list also indicated who would act on the radio, who would do technical work for the videos, etc. When Ms. Finney finished, everybody knew how this next phase fit into the total picture.

At that point the new actors went to Ms. Finney, the new radio directors to Cliff, and the new tech people to me.

The designers and I worked out logistics: who sat where on the "sound stage"; who controlled the microphone; who kept the other students quiet.

As it turned out, most of the designers took turns slamming doors and clicking high heels, but Benny did all the complicated sound effects with his mouth, producing eerily realistic subway noises, rain on windowpanes, etc.

I also told the tech people to take charge—firmly, but gently; they had the responsibility for the tape that would be broadcast throughout the school.

Cliff reminded the new set of writers that the new directors would be boss. But he also allowed the writers to tell the directors their ideas at set intervals. And he explained the importance of the relationship between the director and the technical directors.

Ms. Finney told the actors to pay attention to the words and listen; to let the acting grow out of the text, not preconceived ideas of grand gesture.

All three groups tried to focus as we went through two read-throughs, a session of director notes, and a final "dress rehearsal," but the kids' attention wandered and little fights erupted. Still when we went into the "recording studio," which consisted of a reel-to-reel tape recorder and a good microphone on a large table in the front of the room, the kids worked. The designers turned on the equipment, and life pulsed onto the tape. Some kids dropped lines, others missed emphases, but the momentum carried and we did very few takes on each of the five radio plays.

The broadcasts took place on consecutive Friday afternoons after lunch. As it turned out, that worked out for many of the other teachers, and they praised Ms. Finney's kids. The other classes listened with real attention, looked forward to the next broadcast, and in some cases initiated discussions afterwards. Two classes even sent fan letters to the actors. Of course, little brothers and sisters brought friends to meet the "radio stars" on the playground to get autographs. I had to explain to the neglected writers, directors, and designers that the general audience simply doesn't understand how important they are.

We used the same procedure to prepare the videotaping, which the new tech crew did under Cliff's close supervision. Unfortunately, three things worked against us: a couple of kids missed the early morning rehearsals, so the blocking was rudimentary at best; the kids had difficulty holding their scripts and trying to move about the playing area (the acting space we cleared in the classroom), so they often held the scripts in front of their faces; and the fact that taping stage plays is inherently difficult.

Unedited video takes away the most essential part of theater—the live actors creating and sustaining belief—without replacing it with the fast cuts of film or edited video. An unedited taped play combines the worst elements of both mediums.

(If one wants to do a successful video he should do it the way we did *The Twins in the Lobby*, the video play I showed the first day at P.S. 34. That tape worked because we rehearsed it extensively as a play and then did at least five takes of each scene before it was professionally edited.)

Nevertheless the kids enjoyed the tapes. Seeing themselves and friends "on TV" compensated for the inert productions.

I also told Ms. Finney and Cliff that video can be useful in the rehearsal process. It's invaluable for actors to do a scene, look at a tape, and do the scene again. They can see themselves as the audience sees them and can alter, develop, and expand their performances.

The staged readings proved the only real failures of the process. We simply didn't have time to practice the blocking, and even if we had, eleven- and twelve-year-olds would have had difficulty holding scripts, moving, and acting.

As I thought about it afterwards, I realized that in a staged reading the actors have neither the confidence of memorized lines and blocking, as they do in a full production, nor the freshness and spontaneity they bring to an impromptu reading.

When I offered this opinion to Willie Reale at the 52nd Street Project, he said, "That's why you need professionals," and he offered to recruit four pros to do the "failed" staged readings for the kids.

New adults always interest kids, but the four actors Willie recruited had a special advantage: two had been in a recent miniseries, one was on a soap, and the fourth had done a popular commercial the previous year. They could have come to the school and "winked" at the writing or camped it up or done it mechanically and the kids would have been pleased. But they didn't. They were, in fact, real professionals. They arrived early, organized some basic blocking, and played the material straight, giving performances that any contemporary playwright would have been pleased with. If I had the money, I would have given them a million dollars each.

When I took the class to see *A Chorus Line*, as the fulfillment of my end of the contract, everybody was enthusiastic.

Actually, "enthusiastic" hardly does justice to the scene that day, as we waited in Shubert Alley for the matinee performance: Hector and Jaime raced each other from one end of the alley to the other; Luz studied the various posters on the alley's walls; Saul and Luis tried to sneak in the stage door. Inside, the excitement went to the nth power. Elizabeth seemed to dance in her seat. Kim, Maria Margarita, and Monique (now a threesome) sat rapt and seemed to ingest "Everything's Beautiful at the Ballet" whole. Saul and Luis counted all the lights and peppered me with questions about the technology. Benny and Victor marveled at the mirrors on the set. I had a whole crew of theater lovers with me that day.

Ms. Finney, Cliff, and I met for lunch in Manhattan one Saturday in June. We ate pasta and gossiped about the kids. We also congratulated ourselves. Then we got serious.

Kim's family became the focus of our conversation. Ms. Finney felt we had taken an awful risk. Even now she wondered what consequences would follow.

Cliff took the opposite tack. He felt Kim's situation had been impossible anyway. Doing nothing, pretending it was tenable, was a greater disservice. This way, he reasoned, Kim had grown.

That had been my reasoning, but a sense of responsibility weighed heavily on me. Sitting there with the elegant wine glasses and good linen napkins, I knew I couldn't walk away. I had to make arrangements to keep in contact with Kim.

When I explained that feeling, Ms. Finney said, "Let's keep in touch with all of them," and we were soon planning a barbeque at Ms. Finney's home. Which led me to expound on the 52nd Street Project yet again.

What made the Project so special, aside from all the adult input from professional actors, was the follow-through. Many of the project's kids participated when they lived in midtown hotels. When they moved to the Bronx and Brooklyn, they lived in more stable neighborhoods, but the voices and talents they had been developing would have withered if Willie Reale and Marsue Cumming hadn't followed up, arranged transportation, and made the kids realize that this recreation was not just fun but also a way to express their secret feelings.

Ms. Finney and Cliff seemed interested. All my previous talk about the Project now made sense to them. This kind of an experience should be followed through on. It opened all kinds of possibilities.

That led us to discuss an offer Teachers & Writers had made: we could publish an anthology of the plays. A bound copy of one's own work, together with one's classmates', is a wonderful memento and inspiration. Ms. Finney and Cliff agreed to help me with the typing. We all wanted a permanent record of the experience.

When we said goodby, Ms. Finney confessed that in addition to all this follow-up, she would be teaching playwriting to her new class next year.

Walking down a tree-lined Greenwich Village street the following Friday, I found myself rerunning the plays in my mind. It was a sweet experience — until I remembered that I had to pick up the scripts to type for the anthology before the school closed for the summer.

As I rushed up to the Bronx, I thought about founding my own center, not only to teach theater, but also to work with kids from the time they were seven to seventeen. But how could I make it happen? La Taza de Azul seemed the appropriate place to address that question. I decided to go there right after I picked up the manuscripts.

As soon as I sat down, I knew I had made a mistake. Carmen had the day off. The air conditioner barely cooled. The *cafe con leche* seemed too hot. How could I plan a center under those circumstances? Was I kidding myself?

Distraction seemed to descend towards despair: I suddenly felt incredibly old and tired. How could I build a center? What qualified me to write grant proposals? And even if I took courses on how to get funding, how long would that process take? And what if the economy took a dip, and funds disappeared? And what about space and a reliable staff? And recruiting the kids, becoming accepted in a neighborhood. . . .

And what if I did all that? Would Luz or Kim make a life in the arts? What would happen to Saul and Hiram? And Deana? Would Felix and Hector finish school? I had real hope for Venus, Maria Margarita, William, and Monique. But even they might become mired in the difficulties of growing up in the South Bronx.

Each problem seemed insurmountable, my ambition a delusion. I got up and left.

As I walked to the subway, the streets teemed with people in red and orange tank tops, shorts, and stylish running shoes. The people shouted at each other in rapid Spanish. I just wanted to get home.

"Mr. Sklar, Mr. Sklar!" It was Jaime.

"Hello, Jaime."

"When we gonna do another play?"

"I don't know. It depends on if I get hired to work at your school and. . . ."

"Aww. . . ."

"What are you doing for the summer, Jaime?"

"Nuthin.'"

"No day camp?"

"Naw."

"Maybe you could write another play."

"Would you help me?"

"Well, not this summer. Maybe next year. You see —"

"I gotta go," said Jaime and off he went.

He headed in the direction of the drug supermarket by the school. I followed him for a while. He did not stop to buy or to work as a runner. Most probably he lived nearby and was heading home. I looked at the young men again, lounging dully in the heavy humidity, their hope-lessness resonating off the burned-out building.

I headed for the subway again, but where was I going? To do what? To get another job to pay the rent? And maybe have brief encounters with kids like Jaime? The drug supermarket operated twenty-four hours a day, every day.

I wanted more. I wanted to work with kids all the time. To provide an alternative, an alternative based on what I knew and cared about. I wanted to create that center. Yes, it would be difficult. Yes, it would take time and energy. Yes, it might close before it could show tangible results, if it ever opened in the first place. But, as I stood at the mouth of the subway, I knew I would try.

BRIEF LESSON PLAN

Here is an outline of the twenty basic lessons in this book.

Lesson 1
  A. Change tone: ask "Why write a play?" (pp. 1-2). To focus on honesty about feelings as the source of good playwriting.
  B. Work with feelings: play video, *The Twins in the Lobby* (pp. 2-4). To show how children can write and do related craft jobs, like costumes and make-up, as well as act.

Lesson 2
  A. Change tone.
    1. Create work space (pp. 9-10). To demonstrate how changing the traditional classroom setting stimulates the imagination.
    2. Find spot within space (pp. 10-12). To emphasize the importance of individual feelings within group activities.
  B. Relax body.
    1. Do yoga breathing (pp. 15-17). To relax by working with breath and stretching.
    2. Play stretching game (p. 18). To combine stretching, breathing, and play. Also to create a work ritual.
  C. Listen to senses: play Statues (p. 23). To develop control through a game.
  D. Work with feelings: sound and motion (pp. 29-30). To unite kinetic and emotional impulses.

Lesson 3
  A. Change tone: see lesson 2.
  B. Relax body.
    1. Do breathing II (p. 17). To relax by working with breath and stretching.
    2. Do a hang-out (p. 21). To stretch the spine and related connective tissue.

C. Listen to senses: take imaginary trip to beach (pp. 24-25). To utilize memory and imagination.
D. Work with feelings: improvise.
1. Do messy room conflict (pp. 31-32). To use the imagination and learn to listen.
2. End scene in prose (p. 31). To make the transition from improvisation to writing.
3. Start envelope for student's own book (pp. 38-39, 40). To build a respect for one's own work.

Lesson 4
A. Change tone. See lesson 2.
B. Relax body: take inventory (p. 17). To experience and release all the various muscles of the body.
C. Listen to senses: handle objects (pp. 26-27). To use memory and do mime.
D. Work with feelings: create animal character.
1. Mime animal (pp. 36-37). To work with kinetic sense and imagination.
2. Write a profile (p. 37). To explore the various elements of a character.
3. Write a story (p. 38). To develop a conflict and to work on prose.

Lesson 5
A. Change tone. See lesson 2.
B. Relax body: take inventory (p. 17). To experience and release all the various muscles of the body.
C. Listen to senses. To create a theater piece by combining individual "sounds and motions" (pp. 29-30).
D. Work with feelings: build object character.
1. Play interviewing game (pp. 43-44). To explore a character by responding to questions from fellow students.
2. Do profile (pp. 44-45). See lesson 4.
3. Write story (pp. 45-47). See lesson 4.

Lesson 6
A. Change tone. See lesson 2.

B. Relax body: take inventory and breathe into stomach (p. 18). To release those muscles.

C. Listen to senses: communicate without words (p. 51). To practice paying attention and listening nonverbally.

D. Work with feelings: make nature character.

1. Write profile (pp. 44-45). See lesson 4.

2. Do improvisation (pp. 52-54). See Lesson 3.

3. Work on play format (pp. 53-55). To learn how to put a play on the page correctly.

Lesson 7

A. Change tone. See lesson 2.

B. Relax body: take inventory (p. 17) and breathe into legs. To release those muscles.

C. Senses: play mirrors (p. 60). To control self and concentrate on another actor.

D. Work with feelings: human character I.

1. Write profile—adding job (p. 60). To broaden the profile to include specifically human issues.

2. Do improvisations with most important character (pp. 60-62). To relate improvisations to one's own characters.

3. Create scene in play format (p. 62). To consolidate what was learned in lesson 6D3 (above).

Lesson 8

A. Change tone. See lesson 2.

B. Relax body: take inventory and breathe into area of choice. To release those muscles.

C. Senses: imaginary trip to Brazilian rain forest. See lesson 3.

D. Work with feelings: human character II.

1. Write monologue (pp. 66-68). To write intentions, conflicts, and action in a character's private life.

2. Write dialogue with Special Being (pp. 67-68). To write objectives, conflict, and action between two people.

Lesson 9

A. Change tone. See lesson 2.

B. Relax body: take inventory and breathe into area of choice. To release those muscles.
C. Work with feelings: describe a moment you don't understand.
    1. Self (pp. 73-74). To remember and describe a personal experience.
    2. Observation (p. 74). To remember and describe something you saw or heard.
    3. Dream or fantasy (pp. 74-76). To remember and describe something you dreamed.
    4. What If (p. 76). To imagine in detail and describe.

Lesson 10
A. Change tone. See lesson 2.
B. Relax body: take inventory and breathe into area of choice. To release those muscles.
C. Work with feelings: characters for play.
    1. Write profile—emphasizing fictional names (pp. 80-81). To broaden the profile exercise in lesson 4.
    2. Write a day-in-the-life ending with "objective" (pp. 81-83). To describe a character's typical day in detail.
    3. Draw a picture of character (p. 83). To help visualize the character.

Lessons 11, 12, and 13
A. Change tone. See lesson 2.
B. Relax body: kids lead. To warm up the group and give one child extra responsibility.
C. Work with feelings: writing play.
    1. Starting (pp. 83-84). To get past anxiety and questions and to begin.
    2. Action and beats (pp. 89-90). To learn the structure of a scene.
    3. Write dialogue vs. speech (p. 97). To write characters and scenes, not "reality."
    4. Rewrite (p. 98). To go back over and develop or cut moments for clarity and emphasis.
    5. Titles (p. 99). To choose the best phrase to evoke the piece.
    6. Collaborative writing (p. 91). To work with another writer on a play.

Lessons 14 and 15
A. Change tone. See lesson 2.
B. Relax body: kids lead. See lessons 11, 12, and 13.
C. Work with feelings: reading plays aloud.
 1. Set up logistics of reading (p. 104). To designate readers and set tone for oral presentation.
 2. Choose plays for performance (pp. 103, 105-106, 109-112). To decide which plays should get a full production.
 3. Outline theater protocol (pp. 109-112). To learn how to work with one another in rehearsal.

Lesson 16
A. Change tone. See lesson 2.
B. Relax body: kids lead. See lessons 11, 12, and 13.
C. Work with feelings: directing.
 1. Work with actors (pp. 115-116, 117-118). To create a setting where everybody can work creatively.
 2. "Block" scenes (pp. 116-117). To move characters on the stage.
 3. Create "business" (p. 122). To handle props on the stage.

Lesson 17
A. Change tone. See lesson 2.
B. Relax body: kids lead. See lessons 11, 12, and 13.
C. Work with feelings.
 1. Listen to other actors (pp. 122-124). To respond to the reality of the moment with another actor.
 2. Memorize lines (p. 124). To learn part.
 3. Work with the giggles (pp. 124-125). To control or use nervousness.
 4. Project voice (p. 125). To make yourself heard.

Lesson 18
A. Change tone. See lesson 2.
B. Relax body and listen to senses: kids lead. See lessons 11, 12, and 13.
C. Work with feelings: backstage jobs.
 1. Assign jobs (pp. 129-131). To divide the labor.

2. Enhance the play (pp. 131-132). To use stagecraft to further the author's point.

3. Suggest (pp. 132-133). To create an impression with carefully chosen details.

Lesson 19 (plus as many rehearsals as you can add)

A. Change tone. See lesson 2.

B. Relax body and listen to senses: kids lead. See lessons 11, 12, and 13.

C. Work with feelings.

1. Sign contract (pp. 107-108). To outline responsibilities as well as rights and privileges.

2. Rehearse.

a) Break down scenes (p. 137). To work with a small section of the script at a time.

b) Work scenes (pp. 138-139). To explore different ways of doing the same bit of dialogue.

c) Block scenes (p. 139). To make choices about the movement on the stage.

d) Create "business" (p. 122). To make choices about the props used.

e) Run lines (pp. 139-140). To see if actors know them.

f) Add props, costumes, and set (pp. 140-143). To pull all the elements of a production together.

Lesson 20

A. Relax body and listen to senses: breathe and stretch. To prepare for a performance.

B. Work with feelings: do it all!

GLOSSARY

Beat (or **French scene**): the essential elements of a dramatic scene — characters wanting something from each other, coming into conflict, and taking action.

Blocking: movement on the stage.

Body work: learning how to use the kinetic impulses of one's body for art or physical therapy.

Cinéma vérité: an unedited film that records whatever happens in front of an unmoving camera; a "slice of life."

Creative Dramatics: scenes and plays created spontaneously by actors; often based on folk tales, stories, or personal experiences.

Epic theater: an anti-naturalistic theater technique developed by Bertolt Brecht; designed to make the audience think instead of just feel.

Feet (as in "doing a scene on its feet"): a rehearsal in which the actors try to do a scene with blocking, business, and the lines memorized.

Hang-out: a bending-over exercise that loosens the backbone by gently stretching the connective tissue between the vertebrae.

Important Being: a component of a **profile**; the person or thing the character being profiled cares about most.

Improvisation (or **improv**): a scene that actors make up as they go.

Interviewing game: an exercise in which a child explores a character by responding to questions about the character from fellow students.

Inventory: a technique for slowing down and paying attention to the various muscles, bones, and organs of the body.

Kinetic Awareness: a technique for exploring the kinetic impulses of one's body for awareness, physical therapy, and art.

Method, The: the acting technique developed by Konstantin Stanislavsky and the Moscow Art Theater. The basis of most acting schools in America.

Profile: an exercise designed to help students develop characters bit by bit (name, age, family, wish, fear, etc.)

Rise (as in "at rise"): a term used in play script format; describes what is happening as the curtain rises.

Run lines (as in "to run lines"): actors repeating lines to one another from memory—without affect; often the first stage of a rehearsal.

Sense memory: a technique actors use to discover and transform memories of what they did in response to different temperatures, smells, tastes, etc. An important part of the Method.

Sense work: exercises and games that help develop awareness of sensory experience.

Technical director: the person who oversees all phases of backstage work. Includes lights, sets, props, costumes, make-up, etc.

Technical rehearsal (or a "**tech**"): the rehearsal in which lights, sets, and other technical phases of a production are integrated with acting and directing. Often slow and difficult.

Trip: an exercise in which children explore their senses by imagining the smells, tastes, temperature, etc. of a trip.

Work (as in "to work a section of a script"): the phase of rehearsal when actors try different approaches to a scene.

SELECT BIBLIOGRAPHY

What follows is a purely personal selection of theater books I like and have used over the years.

Personal Accounts

Hart, Moss. *Act I* (New York: Random House, 1959). The autobiography of a Bronx boy who succeeds as a playwright and director. Contains excellent description of Hart's collaboration with George S. Kaufman on *Once in a Lifetime.*

Nef, Hildegard. *The Gift Horse: Report on a Life* (New York: McGraw-Hill, 1971). The autobiography of an actress who lived through the bombing of Berlin as a child, and went on to star on Broadway in *Red Stockings.* A deeply felt and inspiring book.

Williams, Tennessee. *Something Wild* in *Twenty-Seven Wagons Full of Cotton and Other Short Plays* (New York: New Directions, 1953). Williams describes the difficulty, joy, and magic of his first contact with community theater.

Theory

Aristotle. *The Poetics* (New York: Hill and Wang, 1961). Translated by S. H. Butcher. The first description of action, character, conflict, and catharsis as they had been used in ancient Greek theater.

Artaud, Antonin. *The Theater and Its Double* (New York: Grove Press, 1958). Basing his theories on Balinese and other oriental plays, Artaud offers a vision of theater beyond dialogue, explaining how music, dance, and gesture unearth the eternal mysteries.

Stanislavski, Konstantine. *An Actor Prepares* (New York: Theater Arts, 1936). The seminal work on Method Acting. Its narrator, a fictional beginning actor, discovers Stanislavsky's technique under the guidance of a fictional director, who has the wit and style of a Zen master.

Technique

Clurman, Harold. *On Directing* (New York: Macmillan, 1972). A well-organized, clear approach to directing—by a founder of the Group Theater.

Gassner, John. *Producing the Play with the New Scene Technicians Handbook* (New York: The Dryden Press, 1941). Good resource book for set design, lighting, and other theater arts and crafts.

Lawson, John Howard. *The Theory and Technique of Playwriting* (New York: G.P. Putnam, 1936). Lawson integrates the approaches of earlier playwriting theorists like Gustav Freytag, Willam Archer, and George Pierce Baker, and presents them in a clear, satisfying style.

Saltonstall, Ellen. *Kinetic Awareness: Discovering Your Bodymind.* (New York: The Kinetic Awareness Center, 1988). The best account of Elaine Summers' work available. Also provides references to Elsa Gindler (a forerunner of Summers), Moshe Feldenkrais, and Charlotte Selver.

Spolin, Viola. *Improvisation for the Theater* (Evanston, IL: Northwestern University Press, 1987). The definitive theater games book. Story Theater, Second City, and numerous other theater companies use Spolin's approach. Excellent for adults as well as children.

Plays

Brecht, Bertolt. *The Good Person of Szechwan* in *Collected Plays*. Edited by Ralph Mannheim and John Willett (New York: Pantheon, 1970). Modern morality tale told in the style of Brecht's Epic Theater. Also very funny.

Churchill, Caryl. *Cloud Nine* (London: Nick Hern Books, 1989). A truly fresh approach to theater form and content. One of England's best contemporary writers.

Ionesco, Eugene. *The Lesson* in *Four Plays* (New York: Grove Press, 1958). A good example of the Theater of the Absurd.

Lorca, Federico García. *Blood Wedding* in *Three Tragedies* (New York:

New Directions, 1955). A moving, poetic rendering of the conflict between passion and custom. The volume contains *Yerma* and *The House of Bernarda Alba*, two other wonderful Lorca plays.

O'Casey, Sean. *Shadow of a Gun Man* in *Three Plays* (New York: St. Martin's Press, 1957). O'Casey's wonderful characters — usually hilarious and sad — always reveal truth. Volume contains O'Casey's other two classics, *Juno and the Paycock* and *The Plough and the Stars*.

Rabe, David. *Streamers* (New York: Alfred A. Knopf, 1990). Rabe explores the issues of masculinity, social class, and race in an army barracks, and in the process illuminates the Vietnam War and America. One of our best contemporary writers.

Wilson, August. *Fences* (New York: New American Library, 1986). A wrenching story of an African-American man isolating himself from friends and family to survive in the 1950s. Part of a cycle of ten plays in which Wilson explores the development of the African-American community.

Organizations

The Fifty-Second Street Project, 552 W. 52nd St., New York, NY 10017. Offers a unique and successful approach to after-school programming. Includes a special version of Playmaking as well as a whole new approach to adult participation.

The Foundation of the Dramatists Guild, 234 W. 44th St., New York, NY 10036. Sponsors the Young Playwrights Festival, a playwriting contest open to any child in America.

Teachers & Writers Collaborative, 5 Union Square West, New York, NY 10003. Has helped develop the whole notion of artists-in-residence in public schools; current program nurtures an innovative, reciprocal relationship between writers and other artists, full-time teachers, and their schools. Also publishes books on the teaching of imaginative writing.

OTHER T&W PUBLICATIONS OF INTEREST

Making Theater: Developing Plays with Young People by Herbert Kohl. How to develop significant themes through improvisation, how to use dialogue and monologue to help students start writing their own plays, and how to adapt plays and stories for performance. "A leading educator provides valuable and important lessons. A book loaded with specific ideas. Highly recommended" —*Library Materials Guide.*

The Teachers & Writers Handbook of Poetic Forms, edited by Ron Padgett. A clear, concise guide to 74 different poetic forms, their histories, examples, and how to use them. "A treasure" —*Kliatt.*

Personal Fiction Writing: A Guide for Writing from Real Life for Teachers, Students, & Writers by Meredith Sue Willis. "A terrific resource for the classroom teacher as well as the novice writer" —*Harvard Educational Review.*

The Writing Workshop, Vols. 1 & 2 by Alan Ziegler. A perfect combination of theory, practice, and specific assignments. "Invaluable to the writing teacher" —*Contemporary Education.*

Like It Was: A Complete Guide to Writing Oral History by Cynthia Stokes Brown. Particularly good for English and history teachers, but useful for anyone interested in doing oral histories.

The Whole Word Catalogue, Vols. 1 & 2. T&W's best-selling guides to teaching imaginative writing. "*WWC 1* is probably the best practical guide for teachers who really want to stimulate their students to write" —*Learning.* "*WWC 2* is excellent. . . Makes available approaches to the teaching of writing not found in other programs" —*Language Arts.*

For a complete catalogue of T&W books, magazines, audiotapes, videotapes, and computer writing games, contact:
Teachers & Writers Collaborative
5 Union Square West
New York, NY 10003-3306
(212) 691-6590